FREE Test Taking Tips Video/DVD Offer

To better serve you, we created videos covering test taking tips that we want to give you for FREE. **These videos cover world-class tips that will help you succeed on your test.**

We just ask that you send us feedback about this product. Please let us know what you thought about it—whether good, bad, or indifferent.

To get your **FREE videos**, you can use the QR code below or email freevideos@studyguideteam.com with "Free Videos" in the subject line and the following information in the body of the email:

a. The title of your product

b. Your product rating on a scale of 1-5, with 5 being the highest

c. Your feedback about the product

If you have any questions or concerns, please don't hesitate to contact us at info@studyguideteam.com.

Thank you!

Test Prep Books

SCAN HERE

Electrician Apprentice Study Guide

3 Practice Exams & IBEW Aptitude Test Prep Book

[Includes Detailed Answer Explanations]

Joshua Rueda

Written and edited by TPB Publishing.

ISBN 13: 9781637759646
ISBN 10: 1637759649

Table of Contents

Welcome

Dear Reader,

Welcome to your new Test Prep Books study guide! We are pleased that you chose us to help you prepare for your exam. There are many study options to choose from, and we appreciate you choosing us. Studying can be a daunting task, but we have designed a smart, effective study guide to help prepare you for what lies ahead.

Whether you're a parent helping your child learn and grow, a high school student working hard to get into your dream college, or a nursing student studying for a complex exam, we want to help give you the tools you need to succeed. We hope this study guide gives you the skills and the confidence to thrive, and we can't thank you enough for allowing us to be part of your journey.

In an effort to continue to improve our products, we welcome feedback from our customers. We look forward to hearing from you. Suggestions, success stories, and criticisms can all be communicated by emailing us at info@studyguideteam.com.

Sincerely,

Test Prep Books Team

FREE Videos/DVD OFFER

Doing well on your exam requires both knowing the test content and understanding how to use that knowledge to do well on the test. We offer completely FREE test taking tip videos. **These videos cover world-class tips that you can use to succeed on your test.**

To get your **FREE videos**, you can use the QR code below or email freevideos@studyguideteam.com with "Free Videos" in the subject line and the following information in the body of the email:

a. The title of your product
b. Your product rating on a scale of 1-5, with 5 being the highest
c. Your feedback about the product

If you have any questions or concerns, please don't hesitate to contact us at info@studyguideteam.com.

SCAN HERE

Quick Overview

As you draw closer to taking your exam, effective preparation becomes more and more important. Thankfully, you have this study guide to help you get ready. Use this guide to help keep your studying on track and refer to it often.

This study guide contains several key sections that will help you be successful on your exam. The guide contains tips for what you should do the night before and the day of the test. Also included are test-taking tips. Knowing the right information is not always enough. Many well-prepared test takers struggle with exams. These tips will help equip you to accurately read, assess, and answer test questions.

A large part of the guide is devoted to showing you what content to expect on the exam and to helping you better understand that content. In this guide are practice test questions so that you can see how well you have grasped the content. Then, answer explanations are provided so that you can understand why you missed certain questions.

Don't try to cram the night before you take your exam. This is not a wise strategy for a few reasons. First, your retention of the information will be low. Your time would be better used by reviewing information you already know rather than trying to learn a lot of new information. Second, you will likely become stressed as you try to gain a large amount of knowledge in a short amount of time. Third, you will be depriving yourself of sleep. So be sure to go to bed at a reasonable time the night before. Being well-rested helps you focus and remain calm.

Be sure to eat a substantial breakfast the morning of the exam. If you are taking the exam in the afternoon, be sure to have a good lunch as well. Being hungry is distracting and can make it difficult to focus. You have hopefully spent lots of time preparing for the exam. Don't let an empty stomach get in the way of success!

When travelling to the testing center, leave earlier than needed. That way, you have a buffer in case you experience any delays. This will help you remain calm and will keep you from missing your appointment time at the testing center.

Be sure to pace yourself during the exam. Don't try to rush through the exam. There is no need to risk performing poorly on the exam just so you can leave the testing center early. Allow yourself to use all of the allotted time if needed.

Remain positive while taking the exam even if you feel like you are performing poorly. Thinking about the content you should have mastered will not help you perform better on the exam.

Once the exam is complete, take some time to relax. Even if you feel that you need to take the exam again, you will be well served by some down time before you begin studying again. It's often easier to convince yourself to study if you know that it will come with a reward!

Test-Taking Strategies

1. Predicting the Answer

When you feel confident in your preparation for a multiple-choice test, try predicting the answer before reading the answer choices. This is especially useful on questions that test objective factual knowledge. By predicting the answer before reading the available choices, you eliminate the possibility that you will be distracted or led astray by an incorrect answer choice. You will feel more confident in your selection if you read the question, predict the answer, and then find your prediction among the answer choices. After using this strategy, be sure to still read all of the answer choices carefully and completely. If you feel unprepared, you should not attempt to predict the answers. This would be a waste of time and an opportunity for your mind to wander in the wrong direction.

2. Reading the Whole Question

Too often, test takers scan a multiple-choice question, recognize a few familiar words, and immediately jump to the answer choices. Test authors are aware of this common impatience, and they will sometimes prey upon it. For instance, a test author might subtly turn the question into a negative, or he or she might redirect the focus of the question right at the end. The only way to avoid falling into these traps is to read the entirety of the question carefully before reading the answer choices.

3. Looking for Wrong Answers

Long and complicated multiple-choice questions can be intimidating. One way to simplify a difficult multiple-choice question is to eliminate all of the answer choices that are clearly wrong. In most sets of answers, there will be at least one selection that can be dismissed right away. If the test is administered on paper, the test taker could draw a line through it to indicate that it may be ignored; otherwise, the test taker will have to perform this operation mentally or on scratch paper. In either case, once the obviously incorrect answers have been eliminated, the remaining choices may be considered. Sometimes identifying the clearly wrong answers will give the test taker some information about the correct answer. For instance, if one of the remaining answer choices is a direct opposite of one of the eliminated answer choices, it may well be the correct answer. The opposite of obviously wrong is obviously right! Of course, this is not always the case. Some answers are obviously incorrect simply because they are irrelevant to the question being asked. Still, identifying and eliminating some incorrect answer choices is a good way to simplify a multiple-choice question.

4. Don't Overanalyze

Anxious test takers often overanalyze questions. When you are nervous, your brain will often run wild, causing you to make associations and discover clues that don't actually exist. If you feel that this may be a problem for you, do whatever you can to slow down during the test. Try taking a deep breath or counting to ten. As you read and consider the question, restrict yourself to the particular words used by the author. Avoid thought tangents about what the author *really* meant, or what he or she was *trying* to say. The only things that matter on a multiple-choice test are the words that are actually in the question. You must avoid reading too much into a multiple-choice question, or supposing that the writer meant something other than what he or she wrote.

5. No Need for Panic

It is wise to learn as many strategies as possible before taking a multiple-choice test, but it is likely that you will come across a few questions for which you simply don't know the answer. In this situation, avoid panicking. Because most multiple-choice tests include dozens of questions, the relative value of a single wrong answer is small. As much as possible, you should compartmentalize each question on a multiple-choice test. In other words, you should not allow your feelings about one question to affect your success on the others. When you find a question that you either don't understand or don't know how to answer, just take a deep breath and do your best. Read the entire question slowly and carefully. Try rephrasing the question a couple of different ways. Then, read all of the answer choices carefully. After eliminating obviously wrong answers, make a selection and move on to the next question.

6. Confusing Answer Choices

When working on a difficult multiple-choice question, there may be a tendency to focus on the answer choices that are the easiest to understand. Many people, whether consciously or not, gravitate to the answer choices that require the least concentration, knowledge, and memory. This is a mistake. When you come across an answer choice that is confusing, you should give it extra attention. A question might be confusing because you do not know the subject matter to which it refers. If this is the case, don't eliminate the answer before you have affirmatively settled on another. When you come across an answer choice of this type, set it aside as you look at the remaining choices. If you can confidently assert that one of the other choices is correct, you can leave the confusing answer aside. Otherwise, you will need to take a moment to try to better understand the confusing answer choice. Rephrasing is one way to tease out the sense of a confusing answer choice.

7. Your First Instinct

Many people struggle with multiple-choice tests because they overthink the questions. If you have studied sufficiently for the test, you should be prepared to trust your first instinct once you have carefully and completely read the question and all of the answer choices. There is a great deal of research suggesting that the mind can come to the correct conclusion very quickly once it has obtained all of the relevant information. At times, it may seem to you as if your intuition is working faster even than your reasoning mind. This may in fact be true. The knowledge you obtain while studying may be retrieved from your subconscious before you have a chance to work out the associations that support it. Verify your instinct by working out the reasons that it should be trusted.

8. Key Words

Many test takers struggle with multiple-choice questions because they have poor reading comprehension skills. Quickly reading and understanding a multiple-choice question requires a mixture of skill and experience. To help with this, try jotting down a few key words and phrases on a piece of scrap paper. Doing this concentrates the process of reading and forces the mind to weigh the relative importance of the question's parts. In selecting words and phrases to write down, the test taker thinks about the question more deeply and carefully. This is especially true for multiple-choice questions that are preceded by a long prompt.

9. Subtle Negatives

One of the oldest tricks in the multiple-choice test writer's book is to subtly reverse the meaning of a question with a word like *not* or *except*. If you are not paying attention to each word in the question, you can easily be led astray by this trick. For instance, a common question format is, "Which of the following is...?" Obviously, if the question instead is, "Which of the following is not...?," then the answer will be quite different. Even worse, the test makers are aware of the potential for this mistake and will include one answer choice that would be correct if the question were not negated or reversed. A test taker who misses the reversal will find what he or she believes to be a correct answer and will be so confident that he or she will fail to reread the question and discover the original error. The only way to avoid this is to practice a wide variety of multiple-choice questions and to pay close attention to each and every word.

10. Reading Every Answer Choice

It may seem obvious, but you should always read every one of the answer choices! Too many test takers fall into the habit of scanning the question and assuming that they understand the question because they recognize a few key words. From there, they pick the first answer choice that answers the question they believe they have read. Test takers who read all of the answer choices might discover that one of the latter answer choices is actually *more* correct. Moreover, reading all of the answer choices can remind you of facts related to the question that can help you arrive at the correct answer. Sometimes, a misstatement or incorrect detail in one of the latter answer choices will trigger your memory of the subject and will enable you to find the right answer. Failing to read all of the answer choices is like not reading all of the items on a restaurant menu: you might miss out on the perfect choice.

11. Spot the Hedges

One of the keys to success on multiple-choice tests is paying close attention to every word. This is never truer than with words like *almost*, *most*, *some*, and *sometimes*. These words are called "hedges" because they indicate that a statement is not totally true or not true in every place and time. An absolute statement will contain no hedges, but in many subjects, the answers are not always straightforward or absolute. There are always exceptions to the rules in these subjects. For this reason, you should favor those multiple-choice questions that contain hedging language. The presence of qualifying words indicates that the author is taking special care with his or her words, which is certainly important when composing the right answer. After all, there are many ways to be wrong, but there is only one way to be right! For this reason, it is wise to avoid answers that are absolute when taking a multiple-choice test. An absolute answer is one that says things are either all one way or all another. They often include words like *every*, *always*, *best*, and *never*. If you are taking a multiple-choice test in a subject that doesn't lend itself to absolute answers, be on your guard if you see any of these words.

12. Long Answers

In many subject areas, the answers are not simple. As already mentioned, the right answer often requires hedges. Another common feature of the answers to a complex or subjective question are qualifying clauses, which are groups of words that subtly modify the meaning of the sentence. If the question or answer choice describes a rule to which there are exceptions or the subject matter is complicated, ambiguous, or confusing, the correct answer will require many words in order to be expressed clearly and accurately. In essence, you should not be deterred by answer choices that seem excessively long. Oftentimes, the author of the text will not be able to write the correct answer without offering some qualifications and modifications. Your job is to read the answer choices thoroughly and completely and to select the one that most accurately and precisely answers the question.

13. Restating to Understand

Sometimes, a question on a multiple-choice test is difficult not because of what it asks but because of how it is written. If this is the case, restate the question or answer choice in different words. This process serves a couple of important purposes. First, it forces you to concentrate on the core of the question. In order to rephrase the question accurately, you have to understand it well. Rephrasing the question will concentrate your mind on the key words and ideas. Second, it will present the information to your mind in a fresh way. This process may trigger your memory and render some useful scrap of information picked up while studying.

14. True Statements

Sometimes an answer choice will be true in itself, but it does not answer the question. This is one of the main reasons why it is essential to read the question carefully and completely before proceeding to the answer choices. Too often, test takers skip ahead to the answer choices and look for true statements. Having found one of these, they are content to select it without reference to the question above. The savvy test taker will always read the entire question before turning to the answer choices. Then, having settled on a correct answer choice, he or she will refer to the original question and ensure that the selected answer is relevant. The mistake of choosing a correct-but-irrelevant answer choice is especially common on questions related to specific pieces of objective knowledge.

15. No Patterns

One of the more dangerous ideas that circulates about multiple-choice tests is that the correct answers tend to fall into patterns. These erroneous ideas range from a belief that B and C are the most common right answers, to the idea that an unprepared test-taker should answer "A-B-A-C-A-D-A-B-A." It cannot be emphasized enough that pattern-seeking of this type is exactly the WRONG way to approach a multiple-choice test. To begin with, it is highly unlikely that the test maker will plot the correct answers according to some predetermined pattern. The questions are scrambled and delivered in a random order. Furthermore, even if the test maker was following a pattern in the assignation of correct answers, there is no reason why the test taker would know which pattern he or she was using. Any attempt to discern a pattern in the answer choices is a waste of time and a distraction from the real work of taking the test. A test taker would be much better served by extra preparation before the test than by reliance on a pattern in the answers.

Introduction to the IBEW Aptitude Test

Function of the IBEW Aptitude Test

Working together as the Electrical Training Alliance, the International Brotherhood of Electrical Workers (IBEW) and National Electrical Contractors Association (NECA) developed aptitude tests for their respective apprenticeship programs to ensure that prospective electrical apprentices are adequately trained and updated on industry standards. The IBEW Aptitude Test aids the organization in selecting electrician apprentices for its program. The Electrical Training Alliance was previously known as the National Joint Apprenticeship and Training Committee (NJATC), so this exam may also be referred to as the NJATC Aptitude Test.

Test Administration & Format

Candidates who wish to apply to the apprenticeship program must fill out an application form. If he or she meets the basic requirements, access to the free aptitude test will be provided. If the applicant passes the test, they will move on to the next phase of the application process.

The IBEW Aptitude Test is broken down into two smaller tests, the Algebra and Functions Test and the Reading Comprehension Test. It will take approximately two and a half hours to complete both tests, including a short break between subjects. Calculators are not permitted during the test.

The following table demonstrates the question breakdown for each test section:

Test	Questions	Minutes
Algebra and Functions	33	46
Reading Comprehension	36	51

Study Prep Plan for the IBEW Test

1 **Schedule** - Use one of our study schedules below or come up with one of your own.

2 **Relax** - Test anxiety can hurt even the best students. There are many ways to reduce stress. Find the one that works best for you.

3 **Execute** - Once you have a good plan in place, be sure to stick to it.

One Week Study Schedule

Day 1	Algebra and Functions
Day 2	Practical Applications
Day 3	Reading Comprehension
Day 4	Synthesis
Day 5	Practice Tests #1 & #2
Day 6	Practice Test #3
Day 7	Take Your Exam!

Two Week Study Schedule

Day 1	Algebra and Functions	Day 8	Analyzing the Structure of a Text
Day 2	Functions	Day 9	Synthesis
Day 3	Graphs	Day 10	Vocabulary
Day 4	Practical Applications	Day 11	Practice Test #1
Day 5	Average, Median, and Measures of Central Tendency	Day 12	Practice Test #2
Day 6	Reading Comprehension	Day 13	Practice Test #3
Day 7	Rhetoric	Day 14	Take Your Exam!

One Month Study Schedule

Day 1	Algebra and Functions	Day 11	Practice Questions	Day 21	Vocabulary
Day 2	Factoring and Simplifying...	Day 12	Reading Comprehension	Day 22	Finding the Meaning of Words and Phrases in...
Day 3	Functions	Day 13	Identifying Central Ideas or Themes...	Day 23	Practice Questions
Day 4	Solving a Quadratic Equation	Day 14	Summaries of Main Points and Supporting...	Day 24	Practice Test #1
Day 5	Graphs	Day 15	Rhetoric	Day 25	Answer Explanations #1
Day 6	Graphing Solution Sets for Systems of Linear...	Day 16	How an Author's Word Choice Conveys...	Day 26	Practice Test #2
Day 7	Solving Single- and Multistep Problems...	Day 17	Analyzing the Structure of a Text	Day 27	Answer Explanations #2
Day 8	Area, Surface Area, and Volume	Day 18	How the Position and Purpose Shape the Text	Day 28	Practice Test #3
Day 9	Average, Median, and Measures of Central...	Day 19	Synthesis	Day 29	Answer Explanations #3
Day 10	Representing Numbers in Various Ways	Day 20	Asking Questions While Reading	Day 30	Take Your Exam!

Build your own prep plan by visiting:

testprepbooks.com/prep

Algebra and Functions

Algebra

Order of Operations

When solving equations with multiple operations, special rules apply. These rules are known as the **Order of Operations.** The order is as follows: Parentheses, Exponents, Multiplication and Division from left to right, and Addition and Subtraction from left to right. A popular mnemonic device to help remember the order is Please Excuse My Dear Aunt Sally (PEMDAS).

Evaluate the following two problems to understand the Order of Operations:

1) $4 + (3 \times 2)^2 \div 4$

   First, solve the operation within the parentheses: $4 + 6^2 \div 4$.
   Second, solve the exponent: $4 + 36 \div 4$.
   Third, solve the division operation: $4 + 9$.
   Fourth, finish the operation with addition for the answer, 13.

2) $2 \times (6 + 3) \div (2 + 1)^2$

   $2 \times 9 \div (3)^2$
   $2 \times 9 \div 9$
   $18 \div 9$
   2

Solving Linear Equations

When asked to solve a linear equation, it requires determining a numerical value for the unknown variable. Given a linear equation involving addition, subtraction, multiplication, and division, isolation of the variable is done by working backward. Addition and subtraction are inverse operations, as are multiplication and division; therefore, they can be used to cancel each other out.

The first steps to solving linear equations are to distribute if necessary and combine any like terms that are on the same side of the equation. Sides of an equation are separated by an = sign. Next, the equation should be manipulated to get the variable on one side. Whatever is done to one side of an equation, must be done to the other side to remain equal. Then, the variable should be isolated by using inverse operations to undo the order of operations backward. Undo addition and subtraction, then undo multiplication and division.

Algebraically Solving Linear Equations (or Inequalities) in One Variable

Linear equations in one variable and linear inequalities in one variable can be solved following similar processes. Although they typically have one solution, a linear equation can have no solution or can have a solution set of all real numbers. Solution sets for linear inequalities typically consist of an infinite number of values either greater or less than a given value (where the given value may or may not be included in the set). However, a linear inequality can have no solution or can have a solution set consisting of all real numbers.

Linear Equations in One Variable – Special Cases

Solving a linear equation produces a value for the variable that makes the algebraic statement true. If there is no value for the variable that would make the statement true, there is no solution to the equation. Here's a sample equation: $x + 3 = x - 1$. There is no value for *x* in which adding 3 to the value would produce the same result as subtracting 1 from that value. Conversely, if any value for the variable would make a true statement, the equation has an infinite number of solutions. Here's another sample equation:

$$3x + 6 = 3(x + 2)$$

Any real number substituted for *x* would result in a true statement (both sides of the equation are equal).

By manipulating equations similar to the two above, the variable of the equation will cancel out completely. If the constants that are left express a true statement (ex., $6 = 6$), then all real numbers are solutions to the equation. If the constants left express a false statement (ex., $3 = -1$), then there is no solution to the equation.

A question on this material may present a linear equation with an unknown value for either a constant or a coefficient of the variable and ask to determine the value that produces an equation with no solution or infinite solutions. For example:

> $3x + 7 = 3x + 10 + n$; Find the value of *n* that would create an equation with an infinite number of solutions for the variable *x*.

To solve this problem, the equation should be manipulated so the variable *x* will cancel. To do this, 3*x* should be subtracted from both sides, which would leave:

$$7 = 10 + n$$

By subtracting 10 on both sides, it is determined that $n = -3$. Therefore, a value of -3 for *n* would result in an equation with a solution set of all real numbers.

If the same problem asked for the equation to have no solution, the value of *n* would be all real numbers except -3.

Linear Inequalities in One Variable – Special Cases

A linear inequality can have a solution set consisting of all real numbers or can contain no solution. When solved algebraically, a linear inequality in which the variable cancels out and results in a true statement (ex., $7 \geq 2$) has a solution set of all real numbers. A linear inequality in which the variable cancels out and results in a false statement (ex., $7 \leq 2$) has no solution.

Compound Inequalities

A compound inequality is a pair of inequalities joined by *and* or *or*. Given a compound inequality, to determine its solution set, both inequalities should be solved for the given variable. The solution set for a compound inequality containing *and* consists of all the values for the variable that make both inequalities true. If solving the compound inequality results in $x > -9$ and $x \leq 6$, the solution set would consist of all values between -2 and 3, including 3. This may also be written as follows: $-9 < x \leq 6$. Due to the graphs of their solution sets (shown below), compound inequalities such as these are referred to as conjunctions.

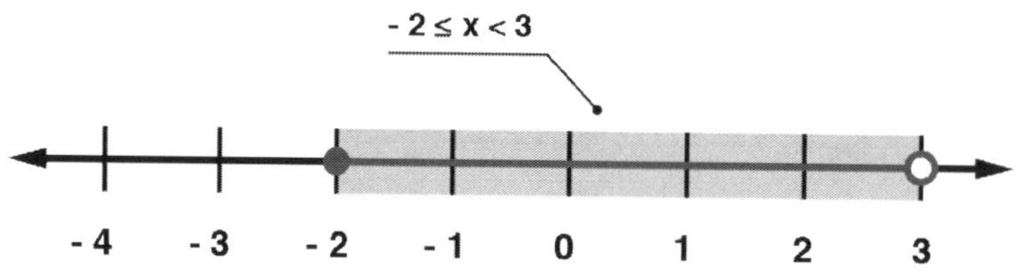

If there are no values that would make both inequalities of a compound inequality containing *and* true, then there is no solution. An example would be $x > 2$ and $x \leq 0$.

The solution set for a compound inequality containing *or* consists of all the values for the variable that make at least one of the inequalities true. The solution set for the compound inequality $x \leq -2$ or $x > 1$ consists of all values less than 2, 6, and all values greater than 6. Due to the graphs of their solution sets (shown below), compound inequalities such as these are referred to as disjunctions.

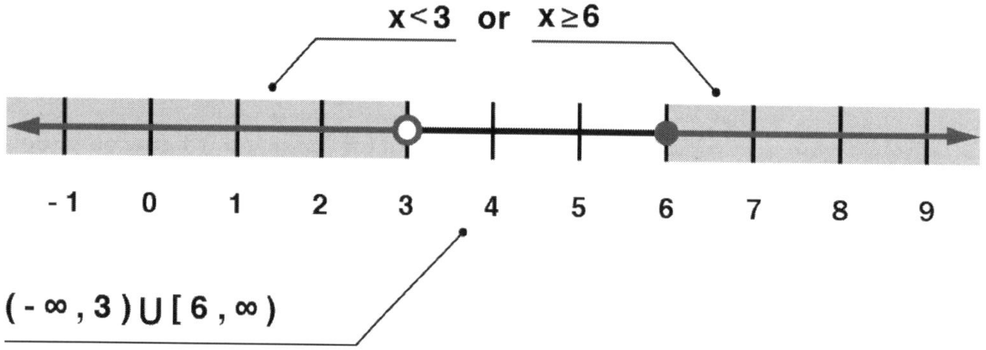

If the two inequalities for a compound inequality containing *or* "overlap," then the solution set contains all real numbers. An example would be $x > 2$ or $x < 7$. Any number would make at least one of these true.

Factoring and Simplifying Polynomials

An expression of the form ax^n, where n is a non-negative integer, is called a **monomial** because it contains one term. A sum of monomials is called a **polynomial**. For example, $-4x^3 + x$ is a polynomial, while $5x^7$ is a monomial. A function equal to a polynomial is called a **polynomial function**.

The monomials in a polynomial are also called the **terms** of the polynomial.

The constants that precede the variables are called **coefficients**.

The highest value of the exponent of x in a polynomial is called the **degree** of the polynomial. So, $-4x^3 + x$ has a degree of 3, while $-2x^5$ in the equation below has a degree of 5:

$$-2x^5 + x^3 + 4x + 1$$

When multiplying polynomials, the degree of the result will be the sum of the degrees of the two polynomials being multiplied.

To add polynomials, add the coefficients of like powers of x. For example,

$$(-2x^5 + x^3 + 4x + 1) + (-4x^3 + x)$$

$$-2x^5 + (1 - 4)x^3 + (4 + 1)x + 1$$

$$-2x^5 - 3x^3 + 5x + 1$$

Likewise, subtraction of polynomials is performed by subtracting coefficients of like powers of x. So,

$$(-2x^5 + x^3 + 4x + 1) - (-4x^3 + x)$$

$$-2x^5 + (1 + 4)x^3 + (4 - 1)x + 1$$

$$-2x^5 + 5x^3 + 3x + 1$$

To multiply two polynomials, multiply each term of the first polynomial by each term of the second polynomial and add the results. For example,

$$(4x^2 + x)(-x^3 + x)$$

$$4x^2(-x^3) + 4x^2(x) + x(-x^3) + x(x)$$

$$-4x^5 + 4x^3 - x^4 + x^2$$

In the case where each polynomial has two terms, like in this example, some students find it helpful to remember this as multiplying the First terms, then the Outer terms, then the Inner terms, and finally the Last terms, with the mnemonic **FOIL**. For longer polynomials, the multiplication process is the same, but there will be, of course, more terms, and there is no common mnemonic to remember each combination.

The process of **factoring** a polynomial means to write the polynomial as a product of other (generally simpler) polynomials. Here is an example:

$$x^2 - 4x + 3 = (x - 1)(x - 3)$$

If a certain monomial divides every term of the polynomial, factor it out of each term, for example:

$$4x^3 + 16x^2 = 4x^2(x + 4).$$

$$x^2 + 2xy + y^2 = (x + y)^2 \text{ or } x^2 - 2xy + y^2 = (x - y)^2$$

$$x^2 - y^2 = (x + y)(x - y)$$

$$x^3 + y^3 = (x + y)(x^2 - xy + y^2)$$

$$x^3 - y^3 = (x - y)(x^2 + xy + y^2)$$

$$x^3 + 3x^2y + 3xy^2 + y^3 = (x + y)^3 \text{ and } x^3 - 3x^2y + 3xy^2 - y^3 = (x - y)^3$$

It sometimes can be necessary to rewrite the polynomial in some clever way before applying the above rules. Consider the problem of factoring $x^4 - 1$. This does not immediately look like any of the cases for which there are rules. However, it's possible to think of this polynomial as:

$$x^4 - 1 = (x^2)^2 - (1^2)^2$$

Now, apply the third rule in the above list to simplify this:

$$(x^2)^2 - (1^2)^2 = (x^2 + 1^2)(x^2 - 1^2) = (x^2 + 1)(x^2 - 1)$$

Factors for polynomials are similar to factors for integers—they are numbers, variables, or polynomials that, when multiplied together, give a product equal to the polynomial in question. One polynomial is a factor of a second polynomial if the second polynomial can be obtained from the first by multiplying by a third polynomial.

$$6x^6 + 13x^4 + 6x^2$$

The above equation can be obtained by multiplying together:

$$(3x^4 + 2x^2)(2x^2 + 3)$$

This means $2x^2 + 3$ and $3x^4 + 2x^2$ are factors of:

$$6x^6 + 13x^4 + 6x^2$$

In general, finding the factors of a polynomial can be tricky. However, there are a few types of polynomials that can be factored in a straightforward way.

If a certain monomial is in each term of a polynomial, it can be factored out. There are several common forms polynomials take, which if you recognize, you can solve. The first example is a perfect square trinomial. To factor this polynomial, first expand the middle term of the expression:

$$x^2 + 2xy + y^2$$

$$x^2 + xy + xy + y^2$$

Factor out a common term in each half of the expression (in this case x from the left and y from the right):

$$x(x + y) + y(x + y)$$

Then the same can be done again, treating $(x + y)$ as the common factor:

$$(x + y)(x + y) = (x + y)^2$$

Therefore, the formula for this polynomial is:

$$x^2 + 2xy + y^2 = (x + y)^2$$

Next is another example of a perfect square trinomial. The process is the similar, but notice the difference in sign:

$$x^2 - 2xy + y^2$$

$$x^2 - xy - xy + y^2$$

Factor out the common term on each side:

$$x(x - y) - y(x - y)$$

Factoring out the common term again:

$$(x - y)(x - y) = (x - y)^2$$

Thus:

$$x^2 - 2xy + y^2 = (x - y)^2$$

The next is known as a difference of squares. This process is effectively the reverse of binomial multiplication:

$$x^2 - y^2$$

$$x^2 - xy + xy - y^2$$

$$x(x - y) + y(x - y)$$

$$(x + y)(x - y)$$

Therefore:

$$x^2 - y^2 = (x + y)(x - y)$$

The following two polynomials are known as the sum or difference of cubes. These are special polynomials that take the form of $x^3 + y^3$ or $x^3 - y^3$. The following formula factors the sum of cubes:

$$x^3 + y^3 = (x + y)(x^2 - xy + y^2)$$

Next is the difference of cubes, but note the change in sign. The formulas for both are similar, but the order of signs for factoring the sum or difference of cubes can be remembered by using the acronym SOAP, which stands for "same, opposite, always positive." The first sign is the same as the sign in the first expression, the second is opposite, and the third is always positive. The next formula factors the difference of cubes:

$$x^3 - y^3 = (x - y)(x^2 + xy + y^2)$$

The following two examples are expansions of cubed binomials. Similarly, these polynomials always follow a pattern:

$$x^3 + 3x^2y + 3xy^2 + y^3 = (x + y)^3$$

$$x^3 - 3x^2y + 3xy^2 - y^3 = (x - y)^3$$

These rules can be used in many combinations with one another. For example, the expression $3x^3 - 24$ has a common factor of 3, which becomes:

$$3(x^3 - 8)$$

A difference of cubes still remains which can then be factored out:

$$3(x - 2)(x^2 + 2x + 4)$$

There are no other terms to be pulled out, so this expression is completely factored.

When factoring polynomials, a good strategy is to multiply the factors to check the result. Let's try another example:

$$4x^3 + 16x^2$$

Both sides of the expression can be divided by 4, and both contain x^2, because $4x^3$ can be thought of as $4x^2(x)$, so the common term can simply be factored out:

$$4x^2(x + 4)$$

It sometimes can be necessary to rewrite the polynomial in some clever way before applying the above rules. Consider the problem of factoring $x^4 - 1$. This does not immediately look like any of the previous polynomials. However, it's possible to think of this polynomial as:

$$x^4 - 1 = (x^2)^2 - (1^2)^2$$

Now, it can be treated as a difference of squares to simplify this:

$$(x^2)^2 - (1^2)^2$$

$$(x^2)^2 - x^2 1^2 + x^2 1^2 - (1^2)^2$$

$$x^2(x^2 - 1^2) + 1^2(x^2 - 1^2)$$

$$(x^2 + 1^2)(x^2 - 1^2)$$

$$(x^2 + 1)(x^2 - 1)$$

Functions

Characteristics of Linear Functions

A **function** is defined as a relationship between inputs and outputs where there is only one output value for a given input. As an example, the following function is in function notation:

$$f(x) = 3x - 4$$

The $f(x)$ represents the output value for an input of x. If $x = 2$, the equation becomes:

$$f(2) = 3(2) - 4 = 6 - 4 = 2$$

The input of 2 yields an output of 2, forming the ordered pair $(2, 2)$. The following set of ordered pairs corresponds to the given function: $(2, 2)$, $(0, -4)$, and $(-2, -10)$. The set of all possible inputs of a function is its **domain**, and all possible outputs is called the **range**. By definition, each member of the domain is paired with only one member of the range.

Functions can also be defined recursively. In this form, they are not defined explicitly in terms of variables. Instead, they are defined using previously-evaluated function outputs, starting with either $f(0)$ or $f(1)$. An example of a recursively-defined function is:

$$f(1) = 2$$

$$f(n) = 2f(n - 1) + 2n$$

$$n > 1$$

The domain of this function is the set of all integers.

Quadratic Equations

A **quadratic equation** can be written in the form:

$$y = ax^2 + bx + c$$

The u-shaped graph of a quadratic function is called a **parabola**. The graph can either open up or open down (upside down u). The graph is symmetric about a vertical line, called the axis of symmetry. Corresponding points on the parabola are directly across from each other (same y-value) and are the same distance from the axis of symmetry (on either side). The axis of symmetry intersects the parabola at its vertex. The y-value of the vertex represents the minimum or maximum value of the function. If the graph opens up, the value of a in its equation is positive, and the vertex represents the minimum of the function.

If the graph opens down, the value of a in its equation is negative, and the vertex represents the maximum of the function.

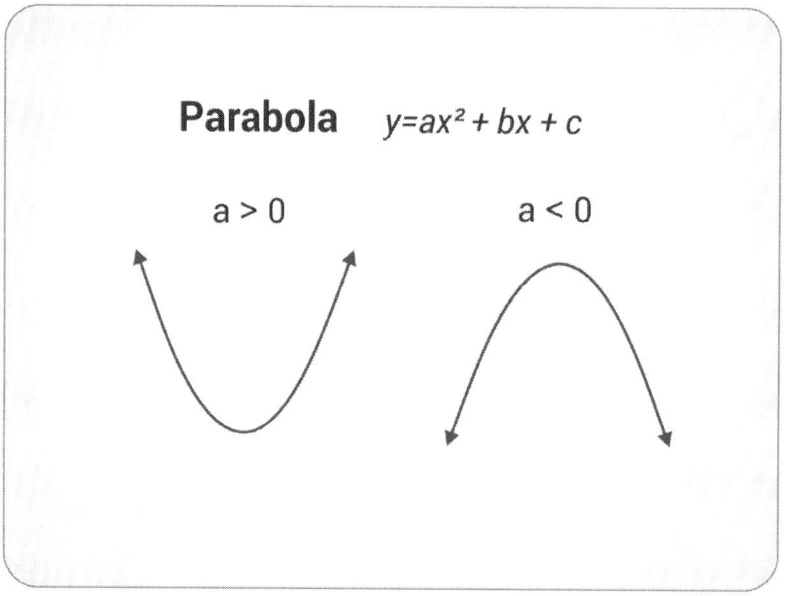

For a quadratic equation where the value of a is positive, as the inputs increase, the outputs increase until a certain value (maximum of the function) is reached. As inputs increase past the value that corresponds with the maximum output, the relationship reverses, and the outputs decrease. For a quadratic equation where a is negative, as the inputs increase, the outputs (1) decrease, (2) reach a maximum, and (3) then increase.

Consider a ball thrown straight up into the air. As time passes, the height of the ball increases until it reaches its maximum height. After reaching the maximum height, as time increases, the height of the ball decreases (it is falling toward the ground). This relationship can be expressed as a quadratic function where time is the input (x) and the height of the ball is the output (y).

To write a quadratic equation that models a real-life scenario, the following is needed: its vertex and any other ordered pair; or any three ordered pairs for the function. Given three ordered pairs, they should be substituted into the general form:

$$y = ax^2 + bx + c$$

This creates a system of three equations. For example, given the ordered pairs $(2, 3)$, $(3, 13)$, and $(4, 29)$, it yields:

$$3 = a(2)2 + b(2) + c \rightarrow 4a + 2b + c = 3$$

$$13 = a(3)2 + b(3) + c \rightarrow 9a + 3b + c = 13$$

$$29 = a(4)2 + b(4) + c \rightarrow 16a + 24b + c = 29$$

The values for a, b, and c in the system can be found and substituted into the general form to write the equation of the function. In this case, the equation is:

$$y = 3x^2 - 5x + 1$$

Given a curve of best-fit that models a quadratic relationship, the equation of the parabola can be written by identifying the vertex of the parabola and another point on the graph. The values for the vertex (h, k) and the point (x, y) should be substituted into the vertex form of a quadratic function to determine the value of a:

$$y = a(x - h)^2 + k$$

To write the equation of a quadratic model with a vertex of $(4, 7)$ and containing the point $(8, 3)$, the values for h, k, x, and y should be substituted into the vertex form of a quadratic equation, resulting in:

$$3 = a(8 - 4)^2 + 7$$

Solving for a, yields $a = -\frac{1}{4}$. Therefore, the equation can be written as:

$$y = -\frac{1}{4}(x - 4)^2 + 7$$

The vertex form can be manipulated in order to write the quadratic equation in standard form.

Solving a Quadratic Equation

A quadratic equation is one in which the highest exponent of the variable is 2. A quadratic equation can have two, one, or zero real solutions. Depending on its structure, a quadratic equation can be solved by (1) factoring, (2) taking square roots, or (3) using the quadratic formula.

Solving Quadratic Equations by Factoring

To solve a quadratic equation by factoring, the equation should first be manipulated to set the quadratic expression equal to zero. Next, the quadratic expression should be factored using the appropriate method(s). Then each factor should be set equal to zero. If two factors multiply to equal zero, then one or both factors must equal zero. Finally, each equation should be solved. Here's a sample:

$$x^2 - 10 = 3x - 6$$

The expression should be set equal to zero:

$$x^2 - 3x - 4 = 0$$

The expression should be factored:

$$(x-4)(x+1)=0$$

Each factor should be set equal to zero:

$$x-4=0; x+1=0$$

Solving yields $x=4$ or $x=-1$.

Solving Quadratic Equations by Taking Square Roots

If a quadratic equation does not have a linear term (variable to the first power), it can be solved by taking square roots. This means x^2 needs to be isolated and then the square root of both sides of the equation should be isolated. There will be two solutions because square roots can be positive or negative. $\sqrt{4}=2$ or -2, because $2 \times 2=4$ and $-2 \times -2=4$.

Here's a sample equation:

$$3x^2-12=0$$

Isolating x^2 yields $x^2=4$. The square root of both sides is then solved: $x=2$ or -2.

The Quadratic Formula

When a quadratic expression cannot be factored or is difficult to factor, the quadratic formula can be used to solve the equation. To do so, the equation must be in the form:

$$ax^2+bx+c=0$$

The quadratic formula is:

$$x=\frac{-b \pm \sqrt{b^2-4ac}}{2a}$$

(The $\pm$ symbol indicates that two calculations are necessary, one using $+$ and one using $-$.) Here's a sample equation:

$$3x^2-2x=3x+2$$

First, the quadratic expression should be set equal to zero:

$$3x^2-5x-2=0$$

Then the values are substituted for a (3), b (-5), and c (-2) into the formula:

$$x=\frac{-(-5) \pm \sqrt{(-5)^2-4(3)(-2)}}{2(3)}$$

Simplification yields:

$$x = \frac{5 \pm \sqrt{49}}{6} \rightarrow x = \frac{5 \pm 7}{6}$$

Calculating two values for x using $+$ and $-$ yields:

$$x = \frac{5 + 7}{6}; x = \frac{5 - 7}{6}$$

Simplification yields:

$$x = 2 \; or \; -\frac{1}{3}$$

Just as with any equation, solutions should be checked by substituting the value into the original equation.

Solving a System of One Linear Equation and One Quadratic Equation

A system of equations consists of two variables in two equations. A solution to the system is an ordered pair (x, y) that makes both equations true. When displayed graphically, a solution to a system is a point of intersection between the graphs of the equations. When a system consists of one linear equation and one quadratic equation, there may be one, two, or no solutions. If the line and parabola intersect at two points, there are two solutions to the system; if they intersect at one point, there is one solution; if they do not intersect, there is no solution.

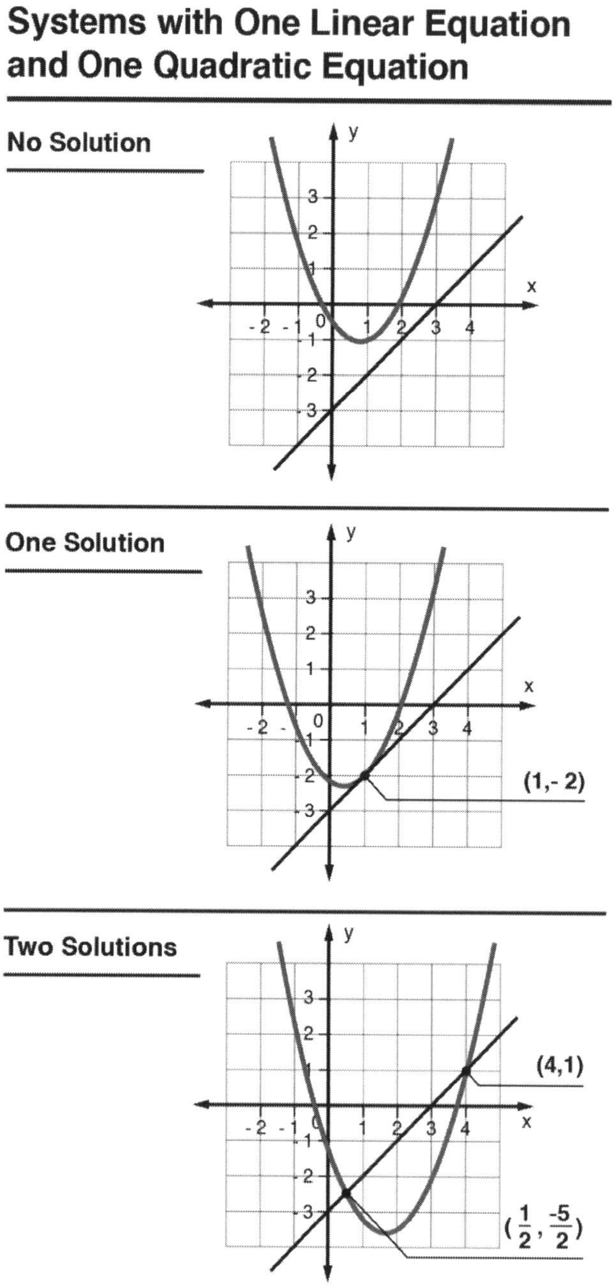

One method for solving a system of one linear equation and one quadratic equation is to graph both functions and identify point(s) of intersection. This, however, is not always practical. Graph paper may not be available, or the intersection points may not be easily identified. Solving the system algebraically involves using the substitution method. Consider the following system:

$$y = x^2 + 9x + 11 \text{ and } y = 2x - 1$$

The equivalent value of y should be substituted from the linear equation $(2x - 1)$ into the quadratic equation. The resulting equation is:

$$2x - 1 = x^2 + 9x + 11$$

Next, this quadratic equation should be solved using the appropriate method: factoring, taking square roots, or using the quadratic formula. Solving this quadratic equation by factoring results in $x = -4$ or $x = -3$. Next, the corresponding y-values should be found by substituting the x-values into the original linear equation:

$$y = 2(-4) - 1; y = 2(-3) - 1$$

The solutions should be written as ordered pairs: $(-4, -9)$ and $(-3, -7)$. Finally, the possible solutions should be checked by substituting each into both of the original equations. In this case, both solutions "check out."

Graphs

As mentioned, a linear equation can be written in the form $y = mx + b$, where x represents the inputs, y represents the outputs, b represents the y-intercept for the graph, and m represents the slope of the line. The y-intercept is the value of y when $x = 0$ and can be thought of as the "starting point." The slope is the rate of change between the variables x and y. A positive slope represents growth, and a negative slope represents decay. Given a table of values for inputs (x) and outputs (y), a linear function would model the relationship if: x and y change at a constant rate per unit interval—for every two inputs a given distance apart, the distance between their corresponding outputs is constant. Here are some sample ordered pairs:

x	0	1	2	3
y	-7	-4	-1	2

For every 1 unit increase in x, y increases by 3 units. Therefore, the change is constant and thus represents linear growth.

Given a scenario involving growth or decay, determining if there is a constant rate of change between inputs (x) and outputs (y) will identify if a linear model is appropriate. A scenario involving distance and time might state that someone is traveling at a rate of 45 miles per hour. For every hour traveled (input), the distance traveled (output) increases by 45 miles. This is a constant rate of change.

Graphing Linear Equations

The simplest equations to graph are the equations whose graphs are lines, called **linear equations**. Every linear equation can be rewritten algebraically so that it looks like:

$$Ax + By = C$$

First, the ratio of the change in the y-coordinate to the change in the x-coordinate is constant for any two distinct points on the line. In any pair of points on a line, two points, (x_1, y_1) and (x_2, y_2)—where $x_1 \neq x_2$—the ratio:

$$\frac{y_2 - y_1}{x_2 - x_1}$$

This will always be the same, even if another pair of points is used.

The following ratio is called the *slope* of the line and is often denoted with the letter m.

$$\frac{y_2 - y_1}{x_2 - x_1}$$

If the slope is **positive**, then the line goes upward when moving to the right. If the slope is **negative**, then it moves downward when moving to the right. If the slope is 0, then the line is **horizontal**, and the y coordinate is constant along the entire line. For lines where the x-coordinate is constant along the entire line, the slope is not defined, and these lines are called **vertical** lines.

The y coordinate of the point where the line touches the y-axis is called the **y-intercept** of the line. It is often denoted by the letter b, used in the form of the linear equation $y = mx + b$. The x coordinate of the point where the line touches the x-axis is called the **x-intercept**. It is also called the *zero* of the line.

Suppose two lines have slopes m_1 and m_2. If the slopes are equal, $m_1 = m_2$, then the lines are **parallel**. Parallel lines never meet one another.

If the below is true then the lines are called **perpendicular** or **orthogonal**.

$$m_1 = -\frac{1}{m_2}$$

Their slopes can also be called opposite reciprocals of each other.

There are several convenient ways to write down linear equations. The common forms are listed here:

- **Standard Form**: $Ax + By = C$, where the slope is given by $\frac{-A}{B}$, and the y-intercept is given by $\frac{C}{B}$.
- **Slope-Intercept Form**: $y = mx + b$, where the slope is m, and the y-intercept is b.
- **Point-Slope Form**: $y - y_1 = m(x - x_1)$, where m is the slope, and (x_1, y_1) is any point on the line.
- **Two-Point Form**: $\frac{y-y_1}{x-x_1} = \frac{y_2-y_1}{x_2-x_1}$, where (x_1, y_1), and (x_2, y_2) are any two distinct points on the line.
- **Intercept Form**: $\frac{x}{x_1} + \frac{y}{y_1} = 1$, where x_1 is the x-intercept, and y_1 is the y-intercept.

Depending upon the given information, different forms of the linear equation can be easier to write down than others. When given two points, the two-point form is easy to write down. If the slope and a single point is known, the point-slope form is easiest to start with. In general, which form to start with depends upon the given information.

Graphing a Line in Slope-Intercept Form

When an equation is written in slope-intercept form, $y = mx + b$, m represents the slope of the line and b represents the y-intercept. The y-intercept is the value of y when $x = 0$ and the point at which the graph of the line crosses the y-axis. The slope is the rate of change between the variables, expressed as a fraction. The fraction expresses the change in y compared to the change in x. If the slope is an integer, it should be written as a fraction with a denominator of 1. For example, 5 would be written as 5/1.

To graph a line given an equation in slope-intercept form, the y-intercept should first be plotted. For example:

$$y = -\frac{2}{3}x + 7$$

To graph the above expression, the y-intercept of 7 would be plotted on the y-axis (vertical axis) at the point $(0, 7)$. Next, the slope would be used to determine a second point for the line. Note that all that is necessary to graph a line is two points on that line. The slope will indicate how to get from one point on the line to another. The slope expresses vertical change (y) compared to horizontal change (x) and therefore is sometimes referred to as $\frac{rise}{run}$. The numerator indicates the change in the y-value (move up for positive integers and move down for negative integers), and the denominator indicates the change in the x-value. For the previous example, using the slope of $-\frac{2}{3}$, from the first point at the y-intercept, the second point should be found by counting down 2 and to the right 3. This point would be located at $(3, 5)$.

T - chart

x	y
0	3
2	0

Intercepts

x - intercept : (2,0)

y - intercept : (0,3)

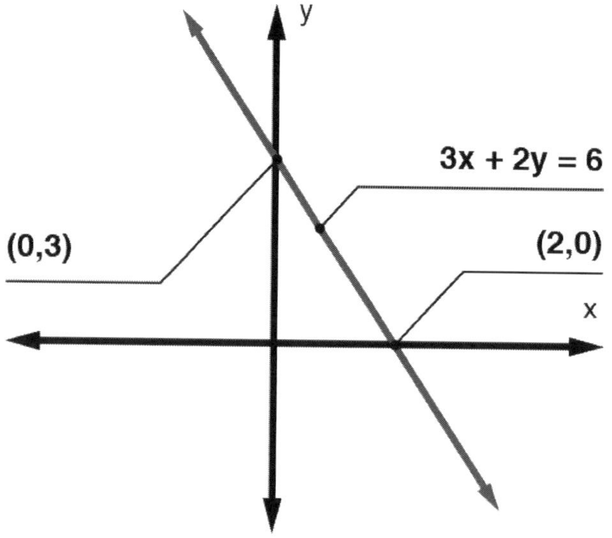

Graphing a Line in Standard Form

It is easy to identify the x- and y-intercepts for the graph of the line when an equation is written in standard form:

$$Ax + By = C$$

Just as the y-intercept is the point at which the line intercepts the y-axis, the x-intercept is the point at which the line intercepts the x-axis. At the y-intercept, $x = 0$; and at the x-intercept, $y = 0$. Given an equation in standard form, $x = 0$ should be used to find the y-intercept.

Likewise, $y = 0$ should be used to find the x-intercept. For example,

$$3x + 2y = 6$$

To graph, change 0 for y. This results in:

$$3x + 2(0) = 6$$

Solving for y yields $x = 2$; therefore, an ordered pair for the line is $(2, 0)$. Substituting 0 for x results in:

$$3(0) + 2y = 6$$

Solving for y yields $y = 3$; therefore, an ordered pair for the line is $(0, 3)$. The two ordered pairs (the x- and y-intercepts) can be plotted and a straight line through them can be constructed.

Writing the Equation of a Line Given its Graph

Given the graph of a line, its equation can be written in two ways. If the y-intercept is easily identified (is an integer), it and another point can be used to determine the slope. When determining $\frac{change\ in\ y}{change\ in\ x}$ from one point to another on the graph, the distance for $\frac{rise}{run}$ is being figured. The equation should be written in slope-intercept form, $y = mx + b$, with m representing the slope and b representing the y-intercept.

The equation of a line can also be written by identifying two points on the graph of the line. To do so, the slope is calculated and then the values are substituted for the slope and either of the ordered pairs into the point-slope form of an equation.

Vertical, Horizontal, Parallel, and Perpendicular Lines

For a vertical line, the value of x remains constant (for all ordered pairs (x, y) on the line, the value of x is the same); therefore, the equations for all vertical lines are written in the form $x = number$. For example, a vertical line that crosses the x-axis at -2 would have an equation of $x = -2$. For a horizontal line, the value of y remains constant; therefore, the equations for all horizontal lines are written in the form $y = number$.

Parallel lines extend in the same exact direction without ever meeting. Their equations have the same slopes and different y-intercepts. For example, given a line with an equation of $y = -3x + 2$, a parallel line would have a slope of -3 and a y-intercept of any value other than 2. Perpendicular lines intersect to form a right angle. Their equations have slopes that are opposite reciprocal (the sign is changed and the fraction is flipped; for example, $-\frac{2}{3}$ and $\frac{3}{2}$) and y-intercepts that may or may not be the same. For example, given a line with an equation of:

$$y = \frac{1}{2}x + 7$$

A perpendicular line would have a slope of $-\frac{2}{1}$ and any value for its y-intercept.

Graphing Solution Sets for Systems of Linear Inequalities in Two Variables

The solution set for a system of inequalities is the region of a graph consisting of ordered pairs that make both inequalities true. To graph the solution set, each linear inequality should first be graphed with appropriate shading. The region of the graph should be identified where the shading for the two inequalities overlaps. This region contains the solution set for the system.

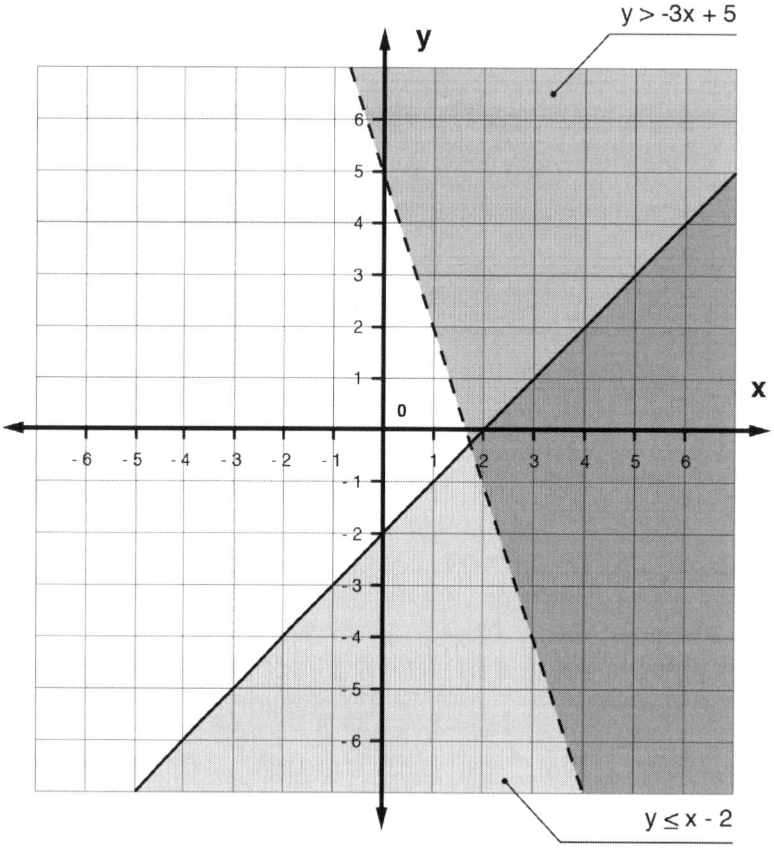

An ordered pair from the region of solutions can be selected to test in the system of inequalities.

Just as with manipulating linear inequalities in one variable, if dividing by a negative number in working with a linear inequality in two variables, the relationship reverses and the inequality sign should be flipped.

Practical Applications

Using Ratios, Rates, Proportions, and Scale Drawings to Solve Single- and Multistep Problems

Ratios, rates, proportions, and scale drawings are used when comparing two quantities. Questions on this material will include expressing relationships in simplest terms and solving for missing quantities.

Ratios

A ratio is a comparison of two quantities that represent separate groups. For example, if a recipe calls for 2 eggs for every 3 cups of milk, it can be expressed as a ratio. Ratios can be written three ways: (1) with the word "to"; (2) using a colon; or (3) as a fraction. For the previous example, the ratio of eggs to cups of milk can be written as: 2 to 3, 2:3, or $\frac{2}{3}$. When writing ratios, the order is important. The ratio of eggs to cups of milk is not the same as the ratio of cups of milk to eggs, 3:2.

In simplest form, both quantities of a ratio should be written as integers. These should also be reduced just as a fraction would be. For example, 5:10 would reduce to 1:2. Given a ratio where one or both quantities are expressed as a decimal or fraction, both should be multiplied by the same number to produce integers. To write the ratio $\frac{1}{3}$ to 2 in simplest form, both quantities should be multiplied by 3. The resulting ratio is 1 to 6.

When a problem involving ratios gives a comparison between two groups, then: (1) a total should be provided and a part should be requested; or (2) a part should be provided and a total should be requested. Consider the following:

> The ratio of boys to girls in the 11th grade is 5:4. If there is a total of 270 11th grade students, how many are girls?

To solve this, the total number of "ratio pieces" first needs to be determined. The total number of 11th grade students is divided into 9 pieces. The ratio of boys to total students is 5:9; and the ratio of girls to total students is 4:9. Knowing the total number of students, the number of girls can be determined by setting up a proportion:

$$\frac{4}{9} = \frac{x}{270}$$

Solving the proportion, it shows that there are 120 11th grade girls.

Rates

A rate is a ratio comparing two quantities expressed in different units. A unit rate is one in which the second is one unit. Rates often include the word *per*. Examples include miles per hour, beats per minute, and price per pound. The word *per* can be represented with a / symbol or abbreviated with the letter "p" and the units abbreviated. For example, miles per hour would be written mi/h. Given a rate that is not in simplest form (second quantity is not one unit), both quantities should be divided by the value of the second quantity. Suppose a patient had 99 heartbeats in 1½ minutes. To determine the heart rate, 1½ should divide both quantities. The result is 66 bpm.

Scale Drawings

Scale drawings are used in designs to model the actual measurements of a real-world object. For example, the blueprint of a house might indicate that it is drawn at a scale of 3 inches to 8 feet. Given one value and asked to determine the width of the house, a proportion should be set up to solve the problem. Given the scale of 3in:8ft and a blueprint width of 1 ft (12 in.), to find the actual width of the building, the proportion $\frac{3}{8} = \frac{12}{x}$ should be used. This results in an actual width of 32 ft.

Proportions

A proportion is a statement consisting of two equal ratios. Proportions will typically give three of four quantities and require solving for the missing value. The key to solving proportions is to set them up properly. Here's a sample problem:

> If 7 gallons of gas costs $14.70, how many gallons can you get for $20?

The information should be written as equal ratios with a variable representing the missing quantity:

$$\left(\frac{gallons}{cost} = \frac{gallons}{cost}\right): \frac{7}{14.70} = \frac{x}{20}$$

To solve, cross multiply (multiply the numerator of the first ratio by the denominator of the second and vice versa) is used, and the products are set equal to each other. Cross-multiplying results in:

$$(7)(20) = (14.7)(x)$$

Solving the equation for *x*, it can be determined that 9.5 gallons of gas can be purchased for $20.

For direct proportions, as one quantity increases, the other quantity also increases. For indirect proportions (also referred to as indirect variations, inverse proportions, or inverse variations), as one quantity increases, the other decreases. Direct proportions can be written:

$$\frac{y_1}{x_1} = \frac{y_2}{x_2}$$

Conversely, indirect proportions are written:

$$y_1 x_1 = y_2 x_2$$

Here's a sample problem:

> It takes 3 carpenters 10 days to build the frame of a house. How long should it take 5 carpenters to build the same frame?

In this scenario, as one quantity increases (number of carpenters), the other decreases (number of days building); therefore, this is an inverse proportion. To solve, the products of the two variables (in this scenario, the total work performed) are set equal to each other ($y_1 x_1 = y_2 x_2$). Using *y* to represent carpenters and *x* to represent days, the resulting equation is:

$$(3)(10) = (5)(x_2)$$

Solving for x_2, it is determined that it should take 5 carpenters 6 days to build the frame of the house.

Solving Single- and Multistep Problems Involving Percentages

The word percent means "per hundred." When dealing with percentages, it may be helpful to think of the number as a value in hundredths. For example, 15% can be expressed as "fifteen hundredths" and written as $\frac{15}{100}$ or .15.

Percent Problems

Material on percentages can include questions such as: What is 15% of 25? What percent of 45 is 3? Five is $\frac{1}{2}$% of what number? To solve these problems, the information should be rewritten as an equation where the following helpful steps are completed: (1) "what" is represented by a variable (*x*); (2) "is" represented by an = sign; and (3) "of" is represented by multiplication. Any values expressed as a percent should be written as a decimal; and if the question is asking for a percent, the answer should be converted accordingly. Here are three sample problems based on the information above:

What is 15% of 25?

$x = .15 \times 25$
$x = 3.75$

What percent of 45 is 3?

$x \times 45 = 3$
$x = 0.0\overline{6}$
$x = 6.\overline{6}\%$

Five is $\frac{1}{2}$% of what number?

$5 = .005 \times x$
$x = 1{,}000$

Percent Increase/Decrease

Problems dealing with percentages may involve an original value, a change in that value, and a percentage change. A problem will provide two pieces of information and ask to find the third. To do so, this formula is used:

$$\frac{change}{original\ value} \text{x } 100 = \text{percent change}$$

Here's a sample problem:

> Attendance at a baseball stadium has dropped 16% from last year. Last year's average attendance was 40,000. What is this year's average attendance?

Using the formula and information, the change is unknown (*x*), the original value is 40,000, and the percent change is 16%. The formula can be written as:

$$\frac{x}{40{,}000} \text{ x } 100 = 16$$

When solving for *x*, it is determined the change was 6,400. The problem asked for this year's average attendance, so to calculate, the change (6,400) is subtracted from last year's attendance (40,000) to determine this year's average attendance is 33,600.

Percent More Than/Less Than

Percentage problems may give a value and what percent that given value is more than or less than an original unknown value. Here's a sample problem:

> A store advertises that all its merchandise has been reduced by 25%. The new price of a pair of shoes is $60. What was the original price?

This problem can be solved by writing a proportion. Two ratios should be written comparing the cost and the percent of the original cost. The new cost is 75% of the original cost (100% - 25%); and the original cost is 100% of the original cost. The unknown original cost can be represented by *x*. The proportion would be set up as: $\frac{60}{75} = \frac{x}{100}$. Solving the proportion, it is determined the original cost was $80.

Solving Single- and Multistep Problems Involving Measurement Quantities, Units, and Unit Conversion

Unit conversions apply to many real-world scenarios, including cooking, measurement, construction, and currency. Problems on this material can be solved similarly to those involving unit rates. Given the conversion rate, it can be written as a fraction (ratio) and multiplied by a quantity in one unit to convert it to the corresponding unit. For example, someone might want to know how many minutes are in 3½ hours. The conversion rate of 60 minutes to 1 hour can be written as:

$$\frac{60\ min}{1\ h}$$

Multiplying the quantity by the conversion rate results in:

$$3\frac{1}{2}h\ \text{x}\frac{60\ min}{1\ h} = 210\ min$$

The "h" unit is canceled. To convert a quantity in minutes to hours, the fraction for the conversion rate would be flipped (to cancel the "min" unit). To convert 195 minutes to hours, the equation $195\ \text{min}\ \text{x}\frac{1h}{60min}$ would be used. The result is $\frac{195h}{60}$, which reduces to $3\frac{1}{4}$ hours.

Converting units may require more than one multiplication. The key is to set up the conversion rates so that units cancel out each other and the desired unit is left. Suppose someone wants to convert 3.25 yards to inches, given that 1yd = 3ft and 12in = 1ft. To calculate, the equation use:

$$3.25yd\ \times\frac{3ft}{1yd}\times\frac{12in}{1ft}$$

The "yd" and "ft" units will cancel, resulting in 117 inches.

Area, Surface Area, and Volume

The area of a two-dimensional figure refers to the number of square units needed to cover the interior region of the figure. This concept is similar to wallpaper covering the flat surface of a wall. For example, if a rectangle has an area of 21 square centimeters (written $21cm^2$), it will take 21 squares, each with sides one centimeter in length, to cover the interior region of the rectangle. Note that area is measured in square units such as: square feet or ft^2; square yards or yd^2; square miles or mi^2.

The surface area of a three-dimensional figure refers to the number of square units needed to cover the entire surface of the figure. This concept is similar to using wrapping paper to completely cover the outside of a box. For example, if a triangular pyramid has a surface area of 17 square inches (written $17in^2$), it will take 17 squares, each with sides one inch in length, to cover the entire surface of the pyramid. Surface area is also measured in square units.

Many three-dimensional figures (solid figures) can be represented by nets consisting of rectangles and triangles. The surface area of such solids can be determined by adding the areas of each of its faces and bases. Finding the surface area using this method requires calculating the areas of rectangles and triangles. To find the area (*A*) of a rectangle, the length (*l*) is multiplied by the width $(w) \rightarrow A = l \times w$. The area of a rectangle with a length of 8cm and a width of 4cm is calculated:

$$A = (8cm) \times (4cm) \rightarrow A = 32cm^2.$$

To calculate the area (*A*) of a triangle, the product of $\frac{1}{2}$, the base (*b*), and the height (*h*) is found:

$$A = \frac{1}{2} \times b \times h$$

Note that the height of a triangle is measured from the base to the vertex opposite of it forming a right angle with the base. The area of a triangle with a base of 11cm and a height of 6cm is calculated:

$$A = \frac{1}{2} \times (11cm) \times (6cm) \rightarrow A = 33cm^2$$

Consider the following triangular prism, which is represented by a net consisting of two triangles and three rectangles.

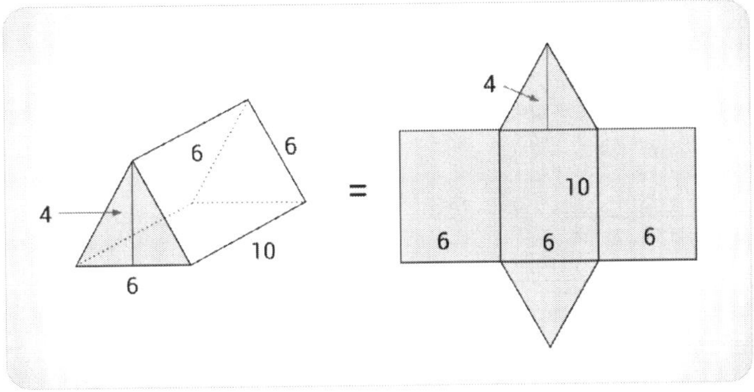

The surface area of the prism can be determined by adding the areas of each of its faces and bases. The surface area (*SA*) = area of triangle + area of triangle + area of rectangle + area of rectangle + area of rectangle.

$$SA = \left(\frac{1}{2} \times b \times h\right) + \left(\frac{1}{2} \times b \times h\right) + (l \times w) + (l \times w) + (l \times w)$$

$$SA = \left(\frac{1}{2} \times 6 \times 4\right) + \left(\frac{1}{2} \times 6 \times 4\right) + (6 \times 10) + (6 \times 10) + (6 \times 10)$$

$$SA = (12) + (12) + (60) + (60) + (60)$$

$$SA = 204 \textit{ square units}$$

Effects of Changes to Dimensions on Area and Volume

Similar polygons are figures that are the same shape but different sizes. Likewise, similar solids are different sizes but are the same shape. In both cases, corresponding angles in the same positions for both figures are congruent (equal), and corresponding sides are proportional in length. For example, the triangles below are similar. The following pairs of corresponding angles are congruent: $\angle A$ and $\angle D$; $\angle B$ and $\angle E$; $\angle C$ and $\angle F$. The corresponding sides are proportional:

$$\frac{AB}{DE} = \frac{6}{3} = 2$$

$$\frac{BC}{EF} = \frac{9}{4.5} = 2$$

$$\frac{CA}{FD} = \frac{10}{5} = 2$$

In other words, triangle *ABC* is the same shape but twice as large as triangle *DEF*.

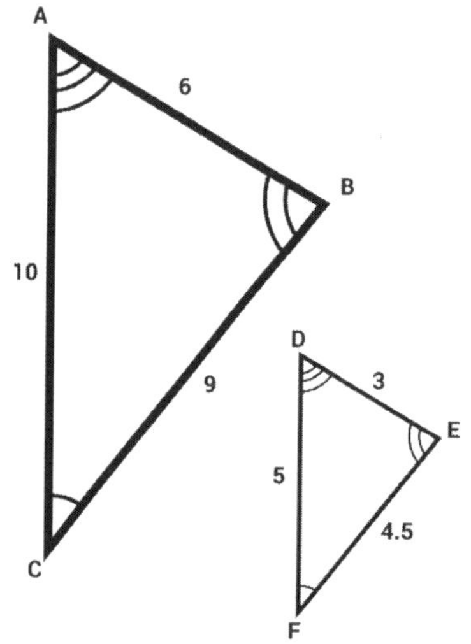

An example of similar triangular pyramids is shown below.

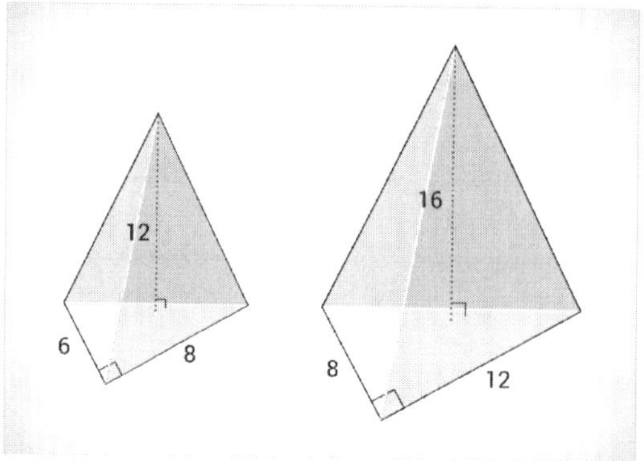

Given the nature of two- and three-dimensional measurements, changing dimensions by a given scale (multiplier) does not change the area of volume by the same scale. Consider a rectangle with a length of 5 centimeters and a width of 4 centimeters. The area of the rectangle is $20cm^2$. Doubling the dimensions of the rectangle (multiplying by a scale factor of 2) to 10 centimeters and 8 centimeters *does*

not double the area to $40cm^2$. Area is a two-dimensional measurement (measured in square units). Therefore, the dimensions are multiplied by a scale that is squared (raised to the second power) to determine the scale of the corresponding areas. For the previous example, the length and width are multiplied by 2. Therefore, the area is multiplied by 2^2, or 4. The area of a 5cm × 4cm rectangle is $20cm^2$. The area of a 10cm × 8cm rectangle is $80cm^2$.

Volume is a three-dimensional measurement, which is measured in cubic units. Therefore, the scale between dimensions of similar solids is cubed (raised to the third power) to determine the scale between their volumes. Consider similar right rectangular prisms: one with a length of 8 inches, a width of 24 inches, and a height of 16 inches; the second with a length of 4 inches, a width of 12 inches, and a height of 8 inches. The first prism, multiplied by a scalar of $\frac{1}{2}$, produces the measurement of the second prism. The volume of the first prism, multiplied by $(\frac{1}{2})^3$, which equals $\frac{1}{8}$, produces the volume of the second prism. The volume of the first prism is 8in × 24in × 16in which equals $3{,}072in^3$. The volume of the second prism is $4in \times 12in \times 8in$ which equals $384in^3$:

$$3{,}072in^3 \times \frac{1}{8} = 384in^3$$

The rules for squaring the scalar for area and cubing the scalar for volume only hold true for similar figures. In other words, if only one dimension is changed (changing the width of a rectangle but not the length) or dimensions are changed at different rates (the length of a prism is doubled and its height is tripled) the figures are not similar (same shape). Therefore, the rules above do not apply.

Average, Median, and Measures of Central Tendency

Suppose that *X* is a set of data points $(x_1, x_2, x_3, \ldots x_n)$, and some description of the general properties of this data need to be found.

The first property that can be defined for this set of data is the **mean**. To find the mean, add up all the data points, then divide by the total number of data points. This can be expressed using **summation notation** as:

$$\bar{X} = \frac{x_1 + x_2 + x_3 + \ldots + x_n}{n} = \frac{1}{n}\sum_{i=1}^{n} x_i$$

For example, suppose that in a class of 10 students, the scores on a test were 50, 60, 65, 65, 75, 80, 85, 85, 90, 100. Therefore, the average test score will be:

$$\frac{1}{10}(50 + 60 + 65 + 65 + 75 + 80 + 85 + 85 + 90 + 100) = 75.5$$

The mean is a useful number if the distribution of data is normal (more on this later), which roughly means that the frequency of different outcomes has a single peak and is roughly equally distributed on both sides of that peak. However, it is less useful in some cases where the data might be split or where there are some **outliers**. Outliers are data points that are far from the rest of the data. For example, suppose there are 10 executives and 90 employees at a company. The executives make $1,000 per hour, and the employees make $10 per hour.

Therefore, the average pay rate will be:

$$\frac{\$1{,}000 \times 10 + \$10 \times 90}{100} = \$109 \text{ per hour}$$

In this case, this average is not very descriptive since it's not close to the actual pay of the executives or the employees.

Another useful measurement is the **median**. In a data set *X* consisting of data points $x_1, x_2, x_3, \ldots x_n$, the median is the point in the middle. The middle refers to the point where half the data comes before it and half comes after, when the data is recorded in numerical order. If *n* is odd, then the median is:

$$x_{\frac{n+1}{2}}$$

If *n* is even, it is defined as:

$$\frac{1}{2}\left(x_{\frac{n}{2}} + x_{\frac{n}{2}+1}\right)$$

It is the mean of the two data points closest to the middle of the data points. In the previous example of test scores, the two middle points are 75 and 80. Since there is no single point, the average of these two scores needs to be found. The average is:

$$\frac{75+80}{2} = 77.5$$

The median is generally a good value to use if there are a few outliers in the data. It prevents those outliers from affecting the "middle" value as much as when using the mean.

Since an outlier is a data point that is far from most of the other data points in a data set, this means an outlier also is any point that is far from the median of the data set. The outliers can have a substantial effect on the mean of a data set, but they usually do not change the median or mode, or do not change them by a large quantity. For example, consider the data set (3, 5, 6, 6, 6, 8). This has a median of 6 and a mode of 6, with a mean of $\frac{34}{6} \approx 5.67$. Now, suppose a new data point of 1,000 is added so that the data set is now (3, 5, 6, 6, 6, 8, 1,000). The median and mode, which are both still 6, remain unchanged. However, the average is now $\frac{1{,}034}{7}$, which is approximately 147.7. In this case, the median and mode will be better descriptions for most of the data points.

The reason for outliers in a given data set is a complicated problem. It is sometimes the result of an error by the experimenter, but often they are perfectly valid data points that must be taken into consideration.

One additional measure to define for *X* is the **mode**. This is the data point that appears more frequently. If two or more data points all tie for the most frequent appearance, then each of them is considered a mode. In the case of the test scores, where the numbers were 50, 60, 65, 65, 75, 80, 85, 85, 90, 100, there are two modes: 65 and 85.

The **first quartile** of a set of data *X* refers to the largest value from the first ¼ of the data points. In practice, there are sometimes slightly different definitions that can be used, such as the median of the first half of the data points (excluding the median itself if there are an odd number of data points). The term also has a slightly different use: when it is said that a data point lies in the first quartile, it means it is less than or equal to the median of the first half of the data points. Conversely, if it lies *at* the first quartile, then it is equal to the first quartile.

When it is said that a data point lies in the **second quartile**, it means it is between the first quartile and the median.

The **third quartile** refers to data that lies between ½ and ¾ of the way through the data set. Again, there are various methods for defining this precisely, but the simplest way is to include all of the data that lie between the median and the median of the top half of the data.

Data that lies in the **fourth quartile** refers to all of the data above the third quartile.

Percentiles may be defined in a similar manner to quartiles. Generally, this is defined in the following manner:

If a data point lies *in* the n-th percentile, this means it lies in the range of the first *n*% of the data.

If a data point lies *at* the *n*-th percentile, then it means that *n*% of the data lies below this data point.

Given a data set *X* consisting of data points $(x_1, x_2, x_3, \dots x_n)$, the **variance of X** is defined to be:

$$\frac{\sum_{i=1}^{n}(x_i - \bar{X})^2}{n}$$

This means that the variance of *X* is the average of the squares of the differences between each data point and the mean of *X*. In the formula, $\bar{X}$ is the mean of the values in the data set, and x_i represents each individual value in the data set. The sigma notation indicates that the sum should be found with n being the number of values to add together. $i = 1$ means that the values should begin with the first value.

Given a data set *X* consisting of data points $(x_1, x_2, x_3, \dots x_n)$, the **standard deviation of X** is defined to be

$$s_x = \sqrt{\frac{\sum_{i=1}^{n}(x_i - \bar{X})^2}{n}}$$

In other words, the standard deviation is the square root of the variance.

Both the variance and the standard deviation are measures of how much the data tend to be spread out. When the standard deviation is low, the data points are mostly clustered around the mean. When the standard deviation is high, this generally indicates that the data are quite spread out, or else that there are a few substantial outliers.

As a simple example, compute the standard deviation for the data set (1, 3, 3, 5). First, compute the mean, which will be:

$$\frac{1+3+3+5}{4} = \frac{12}{4} = 3$$

Now, find the variance of X with the formula:

$$\sum_{i=1}^{4}(x_i - \bar{X})^2 = (1-3)^2 + (3-3)^2 + (3-3)^2 + (5-3)^2$$

$$-2^2 + 0^2 + 0^2 + 2^2 = 8$$

Therefore, the variance is $\frac{8}{4} = 2$. Taking the square root, the standard deviation will be $\sqrt{2}$.

Note that the standard deviation only depends upon the mean, not upon the median or mode(s). Generally, if there are multiple modes that are far apart from one another, the standard deviation will be high. A high standard deviation does not always mean there are multiple modes, however.

Representing Numbers in Various Ways

Concrete Models

Concrete objects are used to develop a tangible understanding of operations of rational numbers. Tools such as tiles, blocks, beads, and hundred charts are used to model problems. For example, a hundred chart (10×10) and beads can be used to model multiplication. If multiplying 5 by 4, beads are placed across 5 rows and down 4 columns producing a product of 20. Similarly, tiles can be used to model division by splitting the total into equal groups. If dividing 12 by 4, 12 tiles are placed one at a time into 4 groups. The result is 4 groups of 3. This is also an effective method for visualizing the concept of remainders.

Representations of objects can be used to expand on the concrete models of operations. Pictures, dots, and tallies can help model these concepts. Utilizing concrete models and representations creates a foundation upon which to build an abstract understanding of the operations.

Rational Numbers on a Number Line

A number line typically consists of integers (...3, 2, 1, 0, -1, -2, -3...), and is used to visually represent the value of a rational number. Each rational number has a distinct position on the line determined by comparing its value with the displayed values on the line. For example, if plotting -1.5 on the number line below, it is necessary to recognize that the value of -1.5 is .5 less than -1 and .5 greater than -2. Therefore, -1.5 is plotted halfway between -1 and -2.

Number lines can also be useful for visualizing sums and differences of rational numbers. Adding a value indicates moving to the right (values increase to the right), and subtracting a value indicates moving to the left (numbers decrease to the left). For example, $-3 - 2$ is displayed by starting at -3 and moving to the left 2 spaces, if the number line is in increments of 1. This will result in an answer of -5.

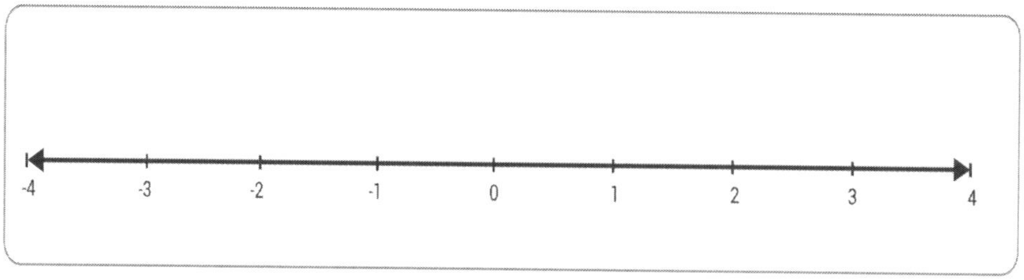

Rectangular Arrays and Area Models

Rectangular arrays include an arrangement of rows and columns that correspond to the factors and display product totals.

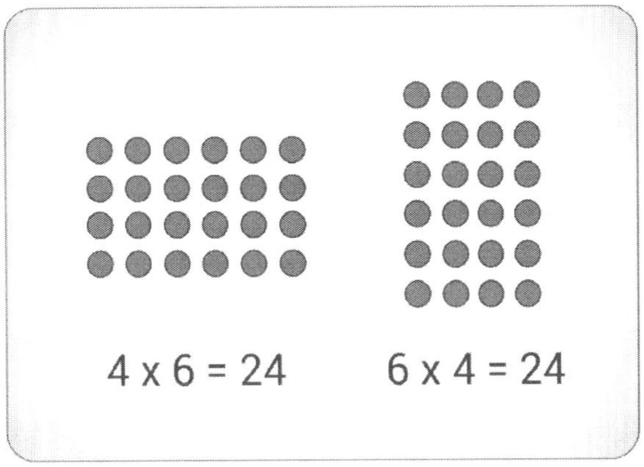

An area model is a rectangle that is divided into rows and columns that match up to the number of place values within each number. For example, $29 \times 65 = 25 + 4$ and $66 = 60 + 5$. The products of those 4 numbers are found within the rectangle and then summed up to get the answer. The entire process is:

$$(60 \times 25) + (5 \times 25) + (60 \times 4) + (5 \times 4)$$

$$1{,}500 + 240 + 125 + 20 = 1{,}885$$

Here is the actual area model:

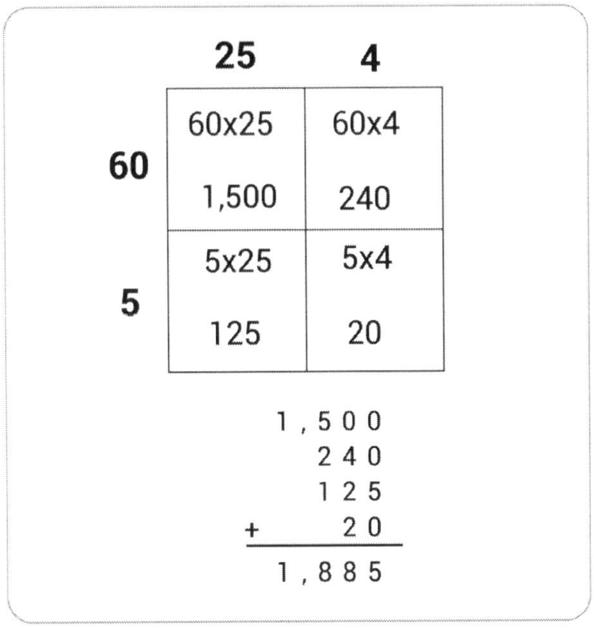

Practice Quiz

1. What is the value of the following expression?

$$\sqrt{8^2 + 6^2}$$

a. 14
b. 10
c. 9
d. 100

2.

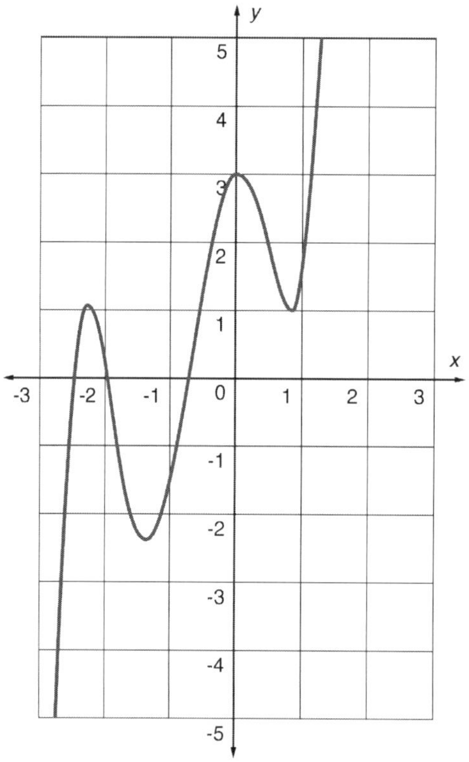

Which of the following functions represents the graph above?

a. $y = x^5 + 3.5x^4 - 6.5x^2 + 0.5x + 3$
b. $y = x^5 - 3.5x^4 + 6.5x^2 - 0.5x - 3$
c. $y = 5x^4 - 6.5x^2 + 0.5x + 3$
d. $y = -5x^4 - 6.5x^2 + 0.5x + 3$

3. If $\log_{10} x = 2$, then *x* is

a. 4
b. 20
c. 100
d. 1,000

4. The graph of which function has an x-intercept of -2?

a. $y = 2x - 3$
b. $y = 4x + 2$
c. $y = x^2 + 5x + 6$
d. $y = -\frac{1}{2} \times 2^x$

5. Karen gets paid a weekly salary and a commission for every sale that she makes. The table below shows the number of sales and her pay for different weeks.

Sales	2	7	4	8
Pay	\$380	\$580	\$460	\$620

Which of the following equations represents Karen's weekly pay?

a. $y = 90x + 200$
b. $y = 90x - 200$
c. $y = 40x + 300$
d. $y = 40x - 300$

See answers on next page.

Answer Explanations

1. B: 8 squared is 64, and 6 squared is 36. These should be added together to get $64 + 36 = 100$. Then, the last step is to find the square root of 100 which is 10.

2. A: The graph contains four turning points (where the curve changes from rising to falling or vice versa). This indicates that the degree of the function (highest exponent for the variable) is 5, eliminating Choices *C* and *D*. The y-intercepts of the functions can be determined by substituting 0 for x and finding the value of y. The function for Choice *A* has a y-intercept of 3, and the function for Choice *B* has a y-intercept of -3. Therefore, Choice *B* is eliminated.

3. C: If $\log_{10} x = 2$, then $10^2 = x$, which equals 100.

4. C: An x-intercept is the point where the graph crosses the x-axis. At this point, the value of y is 0. To determine if an equation has an x-intercept of -2, substitute -2 for x, and calculate the value of y. If the value of -2 for x corresponds with a y-value of 0, then the equation has an x-intercept of -2. The only answer choice that produces this result is Choice *C*:

$$0 = (-2)^2 + 5(-2) + 6$$

5. C: $y = 40x + 300$. In this scenario, the variables are the number of sales and Karen's weekly pay. The weekly pay depends on the number of sales. Therefore, weekly pay is the dependent variable (y), and the number of sales is the independent variable (x). Each pair of values from the table can be written as an ordered pair (*x*, *y*): (2, 380), (7, 580), (4, 460), (8, 620). The ordered pairs can be substituted into the equations to see which creates true statements (both sides equal) for each pair. Even if one ordered pair produces equal values for a given equation, the other three ordered pairs must be checked. The only equation which is true for all four ordered pairs is $y = 40x + 300$:

$$380 = 40(2) + 300 \rightarrow 380 = 380$$

$$580 = 40(7) + 300 \rightarrow 580 = 580$$

$$460 = 40(4) + 300 \rightarrow 460 = 460$$

$$620 = 40(8) + 300 \rightarrow 620 = 620$$

Reading Comprehension

Information and Ideas

Identifying the Main Idea

Topics and main ideas are critical parts of any writing. The **topic** is the subject matter of the piece, and it is a broader, more general term. The **main idea** is what the writer wants to say about that topic. The topic can be expressed in a word or two, but the main idea should be a complete thought.

The topic and main idea are usually easy to recognize in nonfiction writing. An author will likely identify the topic immediately in the first sentence of a passage or essay. The main idea is also typically presented in the introductory paragraph of an essay. In a single passage, the main idea may be identified in the first or the last sentence, but will likely be directly stated and easily recognized by the reader. Because it is not always stated immediately in a passage, it's important to carefully read the entire passage to identify the main idea.

Also remember that when most authors write, they want to make a point or send a message. This point or message of a text is known as the theme. Authors may state themes explicitly, like in *Aesop's Fables*. More often, especially in modern literature, readers must infer the theme based on text details. Usually after carefully reading and analyzing an entire text, the reader can identify the theme. Typically, the longer the piece, the more themes you will encounter, though often one theme dominates the rest, as evidenced by the author's purposeful revisiting of it throughout the passage.

The main idea should not be confused with the thesis statement. A thesis statement is a clear statement of the writer's specific stance, and can often be found in the introduction of a nonfiction piece. The main idea is more of an overview of the entire piece, while the thesis is a specific sentence found in that piece.

In order to illustrate the main idea, a writer will use **supporting details** in a passage. These details can provide evidence or examples to help make a point. Supporting details are most commonly found in nonfiction pieces that seek to inform or persuade the reader.

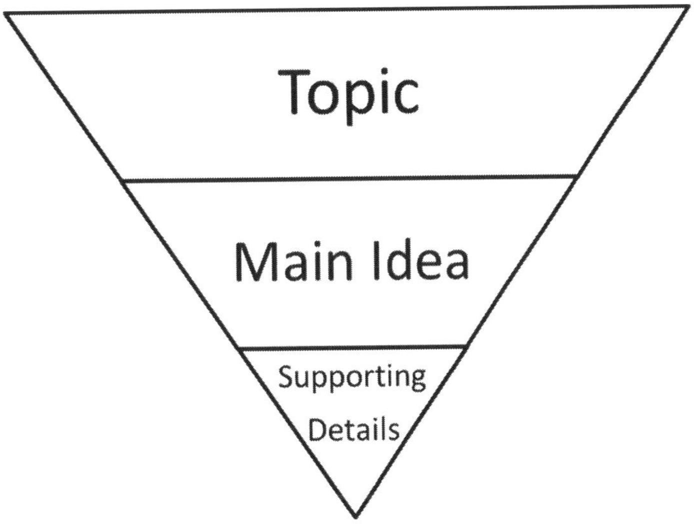

As a reader, you will want to carefully examine the author's supporting details to be sure they are credible. Consider whether they provide evidence of the author's point and whether they directly support the main idea. You might find that an author has used a shocking statistic to grab your attention, but that the statistic doesn't really support the main idea, so it isn't being effectively used in the piece.

Identifying Supporting Details

Supporting details help readers better develop and understand the main idea. Supporting details answer questions like *who, what, where, when, why,* and *how*. Different types of supporting details include examples, facts and statistics, anecdotes, and sensory details.

Persuasive and informative texts often use supporting details. In persuasive texts, authors attempt to make readers agree with their points of view, and supporting details are often used as "selling points." If authors make a statement, they need to support the statement with evidence in order to adequately persuade readers. Informative texts use supporting details such as examples and facts to inform readers. Review the previous "Cheetahs" passage to find examples of supporting details.

Cheetahs

Cheetahs are one of the fastest mammals on the land, reaching up to 70 miles an hour over short distances. Even though cheetahs can run as fast as 70 miles an hour, they usually only have to run half that speed to catch up with their choice of prey. Cheetahs cannot maintain a fast pace over long periods of time because their bodies will overheat. After a chase, cheetahs need to rest for approximately 30 minutes prior to eating or returning to any other activity.

In the example, supporting details include:

- Cheetahs reach up to 70 miles per hour over short distances.
- They usually only have to run half that speed to catch up with their prey.
- Cheetahs will overheat if they exert a high speed over longer distances.
- Cheetahs need to rest for 30 minutes after a chase.

Look at the diagram below (applying the cheetah example) to help determine the hierarchy of topic, main idea, and supporting details.

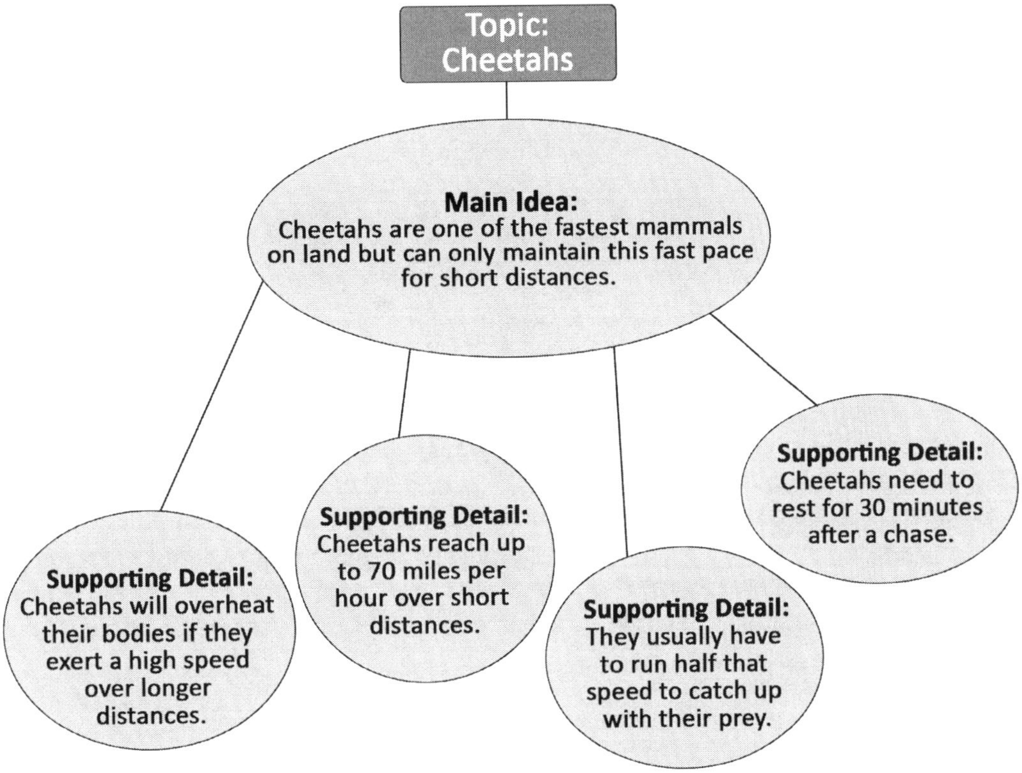

Identifying Central Ideas or Themes of a Text

The **theme** is the central message of a fictional work, whether that work is structured as prose, drama, or poetry. It is the heart of what an author is trying to say to readers through the writing, and theme is largely conveyed through literary elements and techniques.

In literature, a theme can often be determined by considering the overarching narrative conflict within the work. Though there are several types of conflicts and several potential themes within them, the following are the most common:

A. Individual against the self — relevant to themes of self-awareness, internal struggles, pride, coming of age, facing reality, fate, free will, vanity, loss of innocence, loneliness, isolation, fulfillment, failure, and disillusionment

B. Individual against nature — relevant to themes of knowledge vs. ignorance, nature as beauty, quest for discovery, self-preservation, chaos and order, circle of life, death, and destruction of beauty

C. Individual against society — relevant to themes of power, beauty, good, evil, war, class struggle, totalitarianism, role of men/women, wealth, corruption, change vs. tradition, capitalism, destruction, heroism, injustice, and racism

D. Individual against another individual — relevant to themes of hope, loss of love or hope, sacrifice, power, revenge, betrayal, and honor

For example, in Hawthorne's *The Scarlet Letter*, one possible narrative conflict could be the individual against the self, with a relevant theme of internal struggles. This theme is alluded to through characterization—Dimmesdale's moral struggle with his love for Hester and Hester's internal struggles with the truth and her daughter, Pearl. It's also alluded to through plot—Dimmesdale's suicide and Hester helping the very townspeople who initially condemned her.

Sometimes, a text can convey a **message** or **universal lesson**—a truth or insight that the reader infers from the text, based on analysis of the literary and/or poetic elements. This message is often presented as a statement. For example, a potential message in Shakespeare's *Hamlet* could be "Revenge is what ultimately drives the human soul." This message can be immediately determined through plot and characterization in numerous ways, but it can also be determined through the setting of Norway, which is bordering on war.

Authors employ a variety of techniques to present a theme. They may compare or contrast characters, events, places, ideas, or historical or invented settings to speak thematically. They may use analogies, metaphors, similes, allusions, or other literary devices to convey the theme. An author's use of diction, syntax, and tone can also help convey the theme. Authors will often develop themes through the development of characters, use of the setting, repetition of ideas, use of symbols, and through contrasting value systems. Authors of both fiction and nonfiction genres will use a variety of these techniques to develop one or more themes.

Regardless of the literary genre, there are commonalities in how authors, playwrights, and poets develop themes or central ideas.

Authors often do research, the results of which contribute to theme. In prose fiction and drama, this research may include real historical information about the setting the author has chosen or include elements that make fictional characters, settings, and plots seem realistic to the reader. In nonfiction, research is critical since the information contained within this literature must be accurate and, moreover, accurately represented.

In fiction, authors present a narrative conflict that will contribute to the overall theme. In fiction, this conflict may involve the storyline itself and some trouble within characters that needs resolution. In nonfiction, this conflict may be an explanation or commentary on factual people and events.

Authors will sometimes use character motivation to convey theme, such as in the example from *Hamlet* regarding revenge. In fiction, the characters an author creates will think, speak, and act in ways that effectively convey the theme to readers. In nonfiction, the characters are factual, as in a biography, but authors pay particular attention to presenting those motivations to make them clear to readers.

Authors also use literary devices as a means of conveying theme. For example, the use of moon symbolism in Mary Shelley's *Frankenstein* is significant as its phases can be compared to the phases that the Creature undergoes as he struggles with his identity.

The selected point of view can also contribute to a work's theme. The use of first-person point of view in a fiction or non-fiction work engages the reader's response differently than third person point of view. The central idea or theme from a first-person narrative may differ from a third-person limited text.

In literary nonfiction, authors usually identify the purpose of their writing, which differs from fiction, where the general purpose is to entertain. The purpose of nonfiction is usually to inform, persuade, or entertain the audience. The stated purpose of a non-fiction text will drive how the central message or theme, if applicable, is presented.

Authors identify an audience for their writing, which is critical in shaping the theme of the work. For example, the audience for J.K. Rowling's *Harry Potter* series would be different than the audience for a biography of George Washington. The audience an author chooses to address is closely tied to the purpose of the work. The choice of an audience also drives the choice of language and level of diction an author uses. Ultimately, the intended audience determines the level to which that subject matter is presented and the complexity of the theme.

Central Ideas in Informational Texts

Informational text is specifically designed to relate factual information, and although it is open to a reader's interpretation and application of the facts, the structure of the presentation is carefully designed to lead the reader to a particular conclusion or central idea. When reading informational text, it is important that readers are able to understand its organizational structure as the structure often directly relates to an author's intent to inform and/or persuade the reader.

The first step in identifying the text's structure is to determine the thesis or main idea. The thesis statement and organization of a work are closely intertwined. A **thesis statement** indicates the writer's purpose and may include the scope and direction of the text. It may be presented at the beginning of a text or at the end, and it may be explicit or implicit.

Once a reader has a grasp of the thesis or main idea of the text, he or she can better determine its organizational structure. Test takers are advised to read informational text passages more than once in order to comprehend the material fully. It is also helpful to examine any text features present in the text including the table of contents, index, glossary, headings, footnotes, and visuals. The analysis of these features and the information presented within them can offer additional clues about the central idea and structure of a text.

The following questions should be asked when considering structure:

- How does the author assemble the parts to make an effective whole argument?
- Is the passage linear in nature and if so, what is the timeline or thread of logic?
- What is the presented order of events, facts, or arguments? Are these effective in contributing to the author's thesis?
- How can the passage be divided into sections? How are they related to each other and to the main idea or thesis?
- What key terms are used to indicate the organization?

Next, test takers should skim the passage, noting the first line or two of each body paragraph—the **topic sentences**—and the conclusion. Key **transitional terms**, such as *on the other hand, also, because, however, therefore, most importantly*, and *first*, within the text can also signal organizational structure.

Based on these clues, readers should then be able to identify what type of organizational structure is being used. The following organizational structures are most common:

A. **Problem/solution**: organized by an analysis/overview of a problem, followed by potential solution(s)

B. **Cause/effect**: organized by the effects resulting from a cause or the cause(s) of a particular effect

C. **Spatial order**: organized by points that suggest location or direction—e.g., top to bottom, right to left, outside to inside

D. **Chronological/sequence order**: organized by points presented to indicate a passage of time or through purposeful steps/stages

E. **Comparison/contrast**: organized by points that indicate similarities and/or differences between two things or concepts

F. **Order of importance**: organized by priority of points, often most significant to least significant or vice versa

Summaries of Main Points and Supporting Details

Creating an outline that identifies the **main ideas** of a passage as well as the **supporting details** is a helpful tool in effectively summarizing a text. Most outlines will include a title that reveals the topic of the text and is usually a single phrase or word, such as "whales." If the passage is divided up into paragraphs, or the paragraphs into sections, each paragraph or section will have its own main idea. These "main ideas" are usually depicted in outlines as roman numerals. Next, writers use supporting details in order to support or prove the main ideas. The supporting details should be listed underneath each main idea in the outline.

For example:

Title: Whales
I. Killer whales
    a. Highly social
    b. Apex predator
II. Humpback whales
    a. Males produce "song"
    b. Targeted for whaling industry
III. Beluga whales
    a. Complex sense of hearing
    b. Slow swimmers

Making an outline is a useful method of summarization because it forces the reader to deconstruct the text as a whole and to identify only the most important parts of the text.

Ideas from a text can also be organized using graphic organizers. A **graphic organizer** is a way to simplify information and take key points from the text. A graphic organizer such as a timeline may have an event listed for a corresponding date on the timeline while an outline may have an event listed under a key point that occurs in the text. Each reader needs to create the type of graphic organizer that works the best for him or her in terms of being able to recall information from a story. Examples include a **spider-map**, which takes a main idea from the story and places it in a bubble with supporting points branching off the main idea. An **outline** is useful for diagramming the main and supporting points of the entire story, and a **Venn diagram** classifies information as separate or overlapping.

Writing a summary is similar to creating an outline. In both instances, the reader wants to relay the most important parts of the text without being too verbose. A **summary** of a text should begin with stating the main idea of that text. Then, the reader must decide which supporting details are absolutely essential to the main idea of the text and leave any irrelevant information out of the summary. A summary shouldn't be too brief—readers should include important details depicted in the text—but it also shouldn't be too long either. The appeal of a summary to an audience is that they are able to receive the message of the text without being distracted by the style or detours of the author.

Another effective reading comprehension strategy is paraphrasing. Paraphrasing is usually longer than a summary. **Paraphrasing** is taking the author's text and rewriting, or "translating," it into their own words. A tip for paraphrasing is to read a passage over three times. Once you read the passage and understand what the author is saying, cover the original passage and begin to write everything you remember from that passage into your own words. Usually, if you understand the content well enough, you will have translated the main idea of the author into your own words with your own writing style. An effective paraphrase will be as long as the original passage but will have a different writing structure.

Summaries of Informational Texts

Informational text is written material that has the primary function of imparting information about a topic. It is often written by someone with expertise in the topic and directed at an audience that has less knowledge of the topic. Informational texts are written in a different fashion from storytelling or narrative texts. Typically, this type of text has several organizational and structural differences from narrative text. In informational texts, there are features such as charts, graphs, photographs, headings and subheadings, glossaries, indexes, bibliographies, or other guidance features. With the aid of technology, embedded hyperlinks and video content are also sometimes included. Informational material may be written to compare and contrast, be explanatory, link cause and effect, provide opinion, persuade the reader, or serve a number of other purposes. Finally, informational texts typically use a different style of language than narrative texts, which instead, focus more on storytelling.

Making Logical Inferences

Critical readers should be able to make inferences. Making an **inference** requires the reader to read between the lines and look for what is implied rather than what is explicitly stated. That is, using information that *is* known from the text, the reader is able to make a logical assumption about information that is not explicitly stated but is probably true. Read the following passage:

> "Hey, do you wanna meet my new puppy?" Jonathan asked.
>
> "Oh, I'm sorry but please don't—" Jacinta began to protest, but before she could finish Jonathan had already opened the passenger side door of his car and a perfect white ball of fur came bouncing towards Jacinta.

"Isn't he the cutest?" beamed Jonathan.

"Yes—achoo!—he's pretty—aaaachooo!!—adora—aaa—aaaachoo!" Jacinta managed to say in between sneezes. "But if you don't mind, I—I—achoo!—need to go inside."

Which of the following can be inferred from Jacinta's reaction to the puppy?

a. she hates animals
b. she is allergic to dogs
c. she prefers cats to dogs
d. she is angry at Jonathan

An inference requires the reader to consider the information presented and then form their own idea about what is probably true. Based on the details in the passage, what is the best answer to the question? Important details to pay attention to include the tone of Jacinta's dialogue, which is overall polite and apologetic, as well as her reaction itself, which is a long string of sneezes. Answer Choices *A* and *D* both express strong emotions ("hates" and "angry") that are not evident in Jacinta's speech or actions. Answer Choice *C* mentions cats, but there is nothing in the passage to indicate Jacinta's feelings about cats. Answer Choice *B*, "she is allergic to dogs," is the most logical choice—based on the fact that she began sneezing as soon as a fluffy dog approached her, it makes sense to guess that Jacinta might be allergic to dogs. So even though Jacinta never directly states, "Sorry, I'm allergic to dogs!" using the clues in the passage, it is still reasonable to guess that this is true.

Making inferences is crucial for readers of literature, because literary texts often avoid presenting complete and direct information to readers about characters' thoughts or feelings, or they present this information in an unclear way, leaving it up to the reader to interpret clues given in the text. In order to make inferences while reading, readers should ask themselves:

- What details are being presented in the text?
- Is there any important information that seems to be missing?
- Based on the information that the author *does* include, what else is probably true?
- Is this inference reasonable based on what is already known?

Critical Thinking Skills

It's important to read any piece of writing critically. The goal is to discover the point and purpose of what the author is writing about through analysis. It's also crucial to establish the point or stance the author has taken on the topic of the piece. After determining the author's perspective, readers can then more effectively develop their own viewpoints on the subject of the piece.

It is important to distinguish between fact and opinion when reading a piece of writing. A **fact** is information that can be proven true. If information can be disproved, it is not a fact. For example, water freezes at or below thirty-two degrees Fahrenheit. An argument stating that water freezes at seventy degrees Fahrenheit cannot be supported by data and is therefore not a fact. Facts tend to be associated with science, mathematics, and statistics. **Opinions** are information open to debate. Opinions are often tied to subjective concepts like equality, morals, and rights. They can also be controversial.

Authors often use words like *think, feel, believe,* or *in my opinion* when expressing opinion, but these words won't always appear in an opinion piece, especially if it is formally written. An author's opinion may be backed up by facts, which gives it more credibility, but that opinion should not be taken as fact.

A critical reader should be wary of an author's opinion, especially if it is only supported by other opinions.

Fact	Opinion
There are 9 innings in a game of baseball.	Baseball games run too long.
James Garfield was assassinated on July 2, 1881.	James Garfield was a good president.
McDonalds has stores in 118 countries.	McDonalds has the best hamburgers.

Critical readers examine the facts used to support an author's argument. They check the facts against other sources to be sure those facts are correct. They also check the validity of the sources used to be sure those sources are credible, academic, and/or peer-reviewed. Consider that when an author uses another person's opinion to support their argument, even if it is an expert's opinion, it is still only an opinion and should not be taken as fact. A strong argument uses valid, measurable facts to support ideas. Even then, the reader may disagree with the argument as it may be rooted in their personal beliefs.

An authoritative argument may use the facts to sway the reader. Because of this, a writer may choose to only use the information and expert opinion that supports their viewpoint.

If the argument is that wind energy is the best solution, the author will use facts that support this idea. That same author may leave out relevant facts on solar energy. The way the author uses facts can influence the reader, so it's important to consider the facts being used, how those facts are being presented, and what information might be left out.

Critical readers should also look for errors in the argument such as logical fallacies and bias. A **logical fallacy** is a flaw in the logic used to make the argument. Logical fallacies include slippery slope, straw man, and begging the question. Authors can also reflect **bias** if they ignore an opposing viewpoint or present their side in an unbalanced way. A strong argument considers the opposition and finds a way to refute it. Critical readers should look for an unfair or one-sided presentation of the argument and be skeptical, as a bias may be present. Even if this bias is unintentional, if it exists in the writing, the reader should be wary of the validity of the argument.

Readers should also look for the use of **stereotypes**, which refer to specific groups. Stereotypes are often negative connotations about a person or place and should always be avoided. When a critical reader finds stereotypes in a piece of writing, they should immediately be critical of the argument and consider the validity of anything the author presents. Stereotypes reveal a flaw in the writer's thinking and may suggest a lack of knowledge or understanding about the subject.

Rhetoric

Rhetoric is the use of positional or persuasive language to convey one or more central ideas. The idea behind the use of rhetoric is to convince the reader of something. Its use is meant to persuade or motivate the reader. An author may choose to appeal to their audience through logic, emotion, the use of ideology, or by conveying that the central idea is timely, and thus, important to the reader. There are a variety of rhetorical techniques an author can use to achieve this goal.

An author may choose to use traditional elements of style to persuade the reader. They may also use a story's setting, mood, characters, or a central conflict to build emotion in the reader. Similarly, an author may choose to use specific techniques such as alliteration, irony, metaphor, simile, hyperbole, allegory, imagery, onomatopoeia, and personification to persuasively illustrate one or more central ideas they wish the reader to adopt. In order to be successful in a standardized reading comprehension test situation, a reader needs to be well acquainted in recognizing rhetoric and rhetorical devices.

Determining How Ideas or Details Inform the Author's Argument

Once a reader has determined an author's thesis or main idea, he or she will need to understand how textual evidence supports interpretation of that thesis or main idea. Test takers will be asked direct questions regarding an author's main idea and may be asked to identify evidence that would support those ideas. This will require test takers to comprehend literal and figurative meanings within the text passage, be able to draw inferences from provided information, and be able to separate important evidence from minor supporting details. It's often helpful to skim test questions and answer options prior to critically reading informational text; however, test takers should avoid the temptation to solely look for the correct answers. Just trying to find the "right answer" may cause test takers to miss important supporting textual evidence. Making mental note of test questions is only helpful as a guide when reading.

After identifying an author's thesis or main idea, a test taker should look at the supporting details that the author provides to back up their assertions, identifying those additional pieces of information that help expand the thesis. From there, test takers should examine the additional information and related details for credibility, the author's use of outside sources, and be able to point to direct evidence that supports the author's claims. It's also imperative that test takers be able to identify what is strong support and what is merely additional information that is nice to know but not necessary. Being able to make this differentiation will help test takers effectively answer questions regarding an author's use of supporting evidence within informational text.

Identifying Elements of Style

A writer's style is unique. The combinations of elements are carefully designed to create an effect on the reader. For example, the novels of J.K. Rowling are very different in style than the novels of Stephen King, yet both are designed to tell a compelling tale and to entertain readers. Furthermore, the articles found in *National Geographic* are vastly different from those a reader may encounter in *People* magazine, yet both have the same objective: to inform the reader. The difference is in the elements of style.

While there are many elements of style an author can employ, it's important to look at three things: the words they choose to use, the voice an author selects, and the fluency of sentence structure. Word choice is critical in persuasive or pictorial writing. While effective authors will choose words that are succinct, different authors will choose various words based on what they are trying to accomplish. For example, a reader would not expect to encounter the same words in a gothic novel that they would read in a scholastic article on gene therapy. An author whose intent is to paint a picture of a foreboding scene, will choose different words than an author who wants to persuade the reader that a particular political party has the most sound, ideological platform. A romance novelist will sound very different than a true crime writer.

The voice an author selects is also important to note. An author's voice is that element of style that indicates their personality. It's important that authors move us as readers; therefore, they will choose a voice that helps them do that. An author's voice may be satirical or authoritative. It may be light-hearted or serious in tone. It may be silly or humorous as well. Voice, as an element of style, can be vague in nature and difficult to identify, since it's also referred to as an author's tone, but it is that element unique to the author. It is the author's "self." A reader can expect an author's voice to vary across literary genres. A non-fiction author will generally employ a more neutral voice than an author of fiction, but use caution when trying to identify voice. Do not confuse an author's voice with a particular character's voice.

Another critical element of style involves how an author structures their sentences. An effective writer—one who wants to paint a vivid picture or strongly illustrate a central idea—will use a variety of sentence structures and sentence lengths. A reader is more likely to be confused if an author uses choppy, unrelated sentences. Similarly, a reader will become bored and lose interest if an author repeatedly uses the same sentence structure. Good writing is fluent. It flows. Varying sentence structure keeps a reader engaged and helps reading comprehension. Consider the following example:

> The morning started off early. It was bright out. It was just daylight. The moon was still in the sky. He was tired from his sleepless night.

Then consider this text:

> Morning hit hard. He didn't remember the last time light hurt this bad. Sleep had been absent, and the very thought of moving towards the new day seemed like a hurdle he couldn't overcome.

Note the variety in sentence structure. The second passage is more interesting to read because the sentence fluency is more effective. Both passages paint the picture of a central character's reaction to dawn, but the second passage is more effective because it uses a variety of sentences and is more fluent than the first.

Elements of style can also include more recognizable components such as a story's setting, the type of narrative an author chooses, the mood they set, and the character conflicts employed. The ability to effectively understand the use of rhetoric demands the reader take note of an author's word choices, writing voice, and the ease of fluency employed to persuade, entertain, illustrate, or otherwise captivate a reader.

Tone

An author's **tone** is the use of particular words, phrases, and writing style to convey an overall meaning. Tone expresses the author's attitude towards a particular topic. For example, a historical reading passage may begin like the following:

> The presidential election of 1960 ushered in a new era, a new Camelot, a new phase of forward thinking in U.S. politics that embraced brash action and unrest and responded with admirable leadership.

From this opening statement, a reader can draw some conclusions about the author's attitude towards President John F. Kennedy. Furthermore, the reader can make additional, educated guesses about the state of the Union during the 1960 presidential election. By close reading, the test taker can determine that the repeated use of the word *new* and words such as *admirable leadership* indicate the author's tone of admiration regarding President Kennedy's boldness. In addition, the author assesses that the era during President Kennedy's administration was problematic through the use of the words *brash action* and *unrest.* Therefore, if a test taker encountered a test question asking about the author's use of tone and their assessment of the Kennedy administration, the test taker should be able to identify an answer indicating admiration. Similarly, if asked about the state of the Union during the 1960s, a test taker should be able to correctly identify an answer indicating political unrest.

When identifying an author's tone, the following list of words may be helpful. This is not an inclusive list. Generally, parts of speech that indicate attitude will also indicate tone:

- Comical
- Angry
- Ambivalent
- Scary
- Lyrical
- Matter-of-fact
- Judgmental
- Sarcastic
- Malicious
- Objective
- Pessimistic
- Patronizing
- Gloomy
- Instructional
- Satirical
- Formal
- Casual

Message

An author's **message** is the same as the overall meaning of a passage. It is the main idea, or the main concept the author wishes to convey. An author's message may be stated outright, or it may be implied. Regardless, the test taker will need to use careful reading skills to identify an author's message or purpose.

Often, the message of a particular passage can be determined by thinking about why the author wrote the information. Many historical passages are written to inform and to teach readers established, factual information. However, many historical works are also written to convey biased ideas to readers. Gleaning bias from an author's message in a historical passage can be difficult, especially if the reader is presented with a variety of established facts as well. Readers tend to accept historical writing as factual. This is not always the case. Any discerning reader who has tackled historical information on topics such as United States political party agendas can attest that two or more works on the same topic may have completely different messages supporting or refuting the value of the identical policies.

Therefore, it is important to critically assess an author's message separate from factual information. One author, for example, may point to the rise of unorthodox political candidates in an election year based on the failures of the political party in office while another may point to the rise of the same candidates in the same election year based on the current party's successes. The historical facts of what has occurred leading up to an election year are not in refute. Labeling those facts as a failure or a success is a bias within an author's overall message, as is excluding factual information in order to further a particular point. In a standardized testing situation, a reader must be able to critically assess what the author is trying to say separate from the historical facts that surround their message.

Using the example of Lincoln's Gettysburg Address, a test question may ask the following:

> What is the message the author is trying to convey through this address?

Then they will ask the test taker to select an answer that best expresses Lincoln's message to his audience. Based on the options given, a test taker should be able to select the answer expressing the idea that Lincoln's audience should recognize the efforts of those who died in the war as a sacrifice to preserving human equality and self-government.

Effect

The **effect** an author wants to convey is when an author wants to impart a particular mood in their message. An author may want to challenge a reader's intellect, inspire imagination, or spur emotion. An author may present information to appeal to a physical, aesthetic, or transformational sense.

Take the following text as an example:

> In 1963, Martin Luther King stated "I have a dream." The gathering at the Lincoln Memorial was the beginning of the Civil Rights movement and, with its reference to the Emancipation Proclamation, Dr. King's words electrified those who wanted freedom and equality while rising from hatred and slavery. It was the beginning of radical change.

The test taker may be asked about the effect this statement might have on King's audience. Through careful reading of the passage, the test taker should be able to choose an answer that best identifies an effect of grabbing the audience's attention. The historical facts are in place: King made the speech in 1963 at the Lincoln Memorial, kicked off the civil rights movement, and referenced the Emancipation Proclamation. The words *electrified* and *radical change* indicate the effect the author wants the reader to understand as a result of King's speech. In this historical passage, facts are facts. However, the author's message goes beyond the facts to indicate the effect the message had on the audience and, in addition, the effect the event should have on the reader.

How an Author's Word Choice Conveys Attitude and Shapes Meaning, Style, and Tone

Authors choose their words carefully in order to artfully depict meaning, style, and tone, which is most commonly inferred through the use of adjectives and verbs. The **tone** is the predominant emotion present in the text and represents the attitude or feelings that an author has towards a character or event.

To review, an **adjective** is a word used to describe something, and usually precedes the **noun**, a person, place, or object. A **verb** is a word describing an action. For example, the sentence "The scary woodpecker ate the spider" includes the adjective "scary," the noun "woodpecker," and the verb "ate." Reading this sentence may rouse some negative feelings, as the word "scary" carries a negative charge. The **charge** is the emotional connotation that can be derived from the adjectives and verbs and is either positive or negative. Recognizing the charge of a particular sentence or passage is an effective way to understand the meaning and tone the author is trying to convey.

Many authors have conflicting charges within the same text, but a definitive tone can be inferred by understanding the meaning of the charges relative to each other. It's important to recognize key **conjunctions**, or words that link sentences or clauses together. There are several types and subtypes of conjunctions. Three are most important for reading comprehension:

- **Cumulative conjunctions** add one statement to another.
  - Examples: *and, both, also, as well as, not only*
  - e.g. The juice is sweet *and* sour.
- **Adversative conjunctions** are used to contrast two clauses.
  - Examples: *but, while, still, yet, nevertheless*
  - e.g. She was tired, *but* she was happy.
- **Alternative conjunctions** express two alternatives.
  - Examples: *or, either, neither, nor, else, otherwise*
  - e.g. He must eat, *or* he will die.

Identifying the meaning and tone of a text can be accomplished with the following steps:

- Identify the adjectives and verbs.
- Recognize any important conjunctions.
- Label the adjectives and verbs as positive or negative.
- Understand what the charge means about the text.

To demonstrate these steps, examine the following passage from the classic children's poem, "The Sheep":

> Lazy sheep, pray tell me why
>
> In the pleasant fields you lie,
>
> Eating grass, and daisies white,
>
> From the morning till the night?
>
> Everything can something do,
>
> But what kind of use are you?

–Taylor, Jane and Ann. "The Sheep."

This selection is a good example of conflicting charges that work together to express an overall tone. Following the first two steps, identify the adjectives, verbs, and conjunctions within the passage. For this example, the adjectives are <u>underlined</u>, the verbs are in **bold**, and the conjunctions *italicized*:

> <u>Lazy</u> sheep, pray **tell** me why
>
> In the <u>pleasant</u> fields you **lie**,
>
> **Eating** grass, and daisies <u>white,</u>
>
> From the morning till the night?
>
> Everything can something do,
>
> *But* what kind of use are you?

For step three, read the passage and judge whether feelings of positivity or negativity arose. Then assign a charge to each of the words that were outlined. This can be done in a table format, or simply by writing a + or – next to the word.

The word <u>lazy</u> carries a negative connotation; it usually denotes somebody unwilling to work. To **tell** someone something has an exclusively neutral connotation, as it depends on what's being told, which has not yet been revealed at this point, so a charge can be assigned later. The word <u>pleasant</u> is an inherently positive word. To **lie** could be positive or negative depending on the context, but as the subject (the sheep) is lying in a pleasant field, then this is a positive experience. **Eating** is also generally positive.

After labeling the charges for each word, it might be inferred that the tone of this poem is happy and maybe even admiring or innocuously envious. However, notice the adversative conjunction, "but" and what follows. The author has listed all the pleasant things this sheep gets to do all day, but the tone changes when the author asks, "What kind of use are you?" Asking someone to prove their value is a rather hurtful thing to do, as it implies that the person asking the question doesn't believe the subject has any value, so this could be listed under negative charges. Referring back to the verb **tell**, after reading the whole passage, it can be deduced that the author is asking the sheep to tell what use the sheep is, so this has a negative charge.

+	–
• Pleasant • Lie in fields • From morning to night	• Lazy • Tell me • What kind of use are you

Upon examining the charges, it might seem like there's an even amount of positive and negative emotion in this selection, and that's where the conjunction "but" becomes crucial to identifying the tone. The conjunction "but" indicates there's a contrasting view to the pleasantness of the sheep's daily life, and this view is that the sheep is lazy and useless, which is also indicated by the first line, "lazy sheep, pray tell me why."

It might be helpful to look at questions pertaining to tone. For this selection, consider the following question:

The author of the poem regards the sheep with a feeling of what?

a. Respect
b. Disgust
c. Apprehension
d. Intrigue

Considering the author views the sheep as lazy with nothing to offer, Choice *A* appears to reflect the opposite of what the author is feeling.

Choice *B* seems to mirror the author's feelings towards the sheep, as laziness is considered a disreputable trait, and people (or personified animals, in this case) with unfavorable traits might be viewed with disgust.

Choice *C* doesn't make sense within context, as laziness isn't usually feared.

Choice *D* is tricky, as it may be tempting to argue that the author is intrigued with the sheep because they ask, "pray tell me why." This is another out-of-scope answer choice as it doesn't *quite* describe the feelings the author experiences and there's also a much better fit in Choice *B*.

An author's choice of words—also referred to as **diction**—helps to convey meaning in a particular way. Through diction, an author can convey a particular tone—e.g., a humorous tone, a serious tone—in order to support the thesis in a meaningful way to the reader.

Connotation and Denotation

Connotation is when an author chooses words or phrases that invoke ideas or feelings other than their literal meaning. An example of the use of connotation is the word *cheap*, which suggests something is poor in value or negatively describes a person as reluctant to spend money. When something or someone is described this way, the reader is more inclined to have a particular image or feeling. Thus, connotation can be a very effective language tool in creating emotion and swaying opinion. However, connotations are sometimes hard to pin down because varying emotions can be associated with a word. Generally, though, connotative meanings tend to be fairly consistent within a specific cultural group.

Denotation refers to words or phrases that mean exactly what they say. It is helpful when a writer wants to present hard facts or vocabulary terms with which readers may be unfamiliar. Some examples of denotation are the words *inexpensive* and *frugal*. *Inexpensive* refers to the cost of something, not its value, and *frugal* indicates that a person is conscientiously watching their spending. These terms do not elicit the same emotions that *cheap* does.

Authors sometimes choose to use both, but what they choose and when they use it is what critical readers need to differentiate. One method isn't inherently better than the other; however, one may create a better effect, depending upon an author's intent. If, for example, an author's purpose is to inform, to instruct, and to familiarize readers with a difficult subject, their use of connotation may be helpful. However, it may also undermine credibility and confuse readers. An author who wants to create a credible, scholarly effect in their text would most likely use denotation, which emphasizes literal, factual meaning and examples.

Technical Language

Test takers and critical readers alike should be very aware of technical language used within informational text. **Technical language** refers to terminology that is specific to a particular industry and is best understood by those specializing in that industry. This language is fairly easy to differentiate since it will most likely be unfamiliar to readers. It's critical to be able to define technical language either by the author's written definition, through the use of an included glossary—if offered—or through context clues that help readers clarify word meaning.

Analyzing the Structure of a Text

Good writing is not merely a random collection of sentences. No matter how well written, sentences must relate and coordinate appropriately with one another. If not, the writing seems random, haphazard, and disorganized. Therefore, good writing must be organized, where each sentence fits a larger context and relates to the sentences around it.

Transition Words

The writer should act as a guide, showing the reader how all the sentences fit together. Consider this seat belt example:

> Seat belts save more lives than any other automobile safety feature. Many studies show that airbags save lives as well. Not all cars have airbags. Many older cars don't. Air bags aren't entirely reliable. Studies show that in 15% of accidents, airbags don't deploy as designed. Seat belt malfunctions are extremely rare.

There's nothing wrong with any of these sentences individually, but together they're disjointed and difficult to follow. The best way for the writer to communicate information is through the use of transition words. Here are examples of transition words and phrases that tie sentences together, enabling a more natural flow:

> To show causality: *as a result, therefore*, and *consequently*
> To compare and contrast: *however, but,* and *on the other hand*
> To introduce examples: *for instance, namely,* and *including*
> To show order of importance: *foremost, primarily, secondly,* and *lastly*

Note that this is not a complete list of transitions. There are many more that can be used; however, most fit into these or similar categories. The important point is that the words should clearly show the relationship between sentences, supporting information, and the main idea.

Here is an update to the previous example using transition words. These changes make it easier to read and bring clarity to the writer's points:

> Seat belts save more lives than any other automobile safety feature. Many studies show that airbags save lives as well; however, not all cars have airbags. For instance, some older cars don't. Furthermore, air bags aren't entirely reliable. For example, studies show that in 15% of accidents, airbags don't deploy as designed, but, on the other hand, seat belt malfunctions are extremely rare.

Also, test takers should be prepared to analyze whether the writer is using the best transition word or phrase for the situation. For example, the sentence: "As a result, seat belt malfunctions are extremely rare" doesn't make sense in the context above because the writer is trying to show the contrast between seat belts and airbags, not the causality.

Logical Sequence

Even if the writer includes plenty of information to support their point, the writing is only coherent when the information is in a logical order. First, the writer should introduce the main idea, whether for a paragraph, a section, or the entire piece. Second, they should present evidence to support the main idea by using transitional language. This shows the reader how the information relates to the main idea and to the sentences around it. The writer should then take time to interpret the information, making sure necessary connections are obvious to the reader. Finally, the writer can summarize the information in a closing section.

Though most writing follows this pattern, it isn't a set rule. Sometimes writers change the order for effect. For example, the writer can begin with a surprising piece of supporting information to grab the reader's attention, and then transition to the main idea. Thus, if a passage doesn't follow the logical order, don't immediately assume it's wrong. However, most writing usually settles into a logical sequence after a nontraditional beginning.

Introductions and Conclusions

Examining the writer's strategies for introductions and conclusions puts the reader in the right mindset to interpret the rest of the text. Look for methods the writer might use for introductions such as:

> Stating the main point immediately, followed by outlining how the rest of the piece supports this claim.
>
> Establishing important, smaller pieces of the main idea first, and then grouping these points into a case for the main idea.
>
> Opening with a quotation, anecdote, question, seeming paradox, or other piece of interesting information, and then using it to lead to the main point.

Whatever method the writer chooses, the introduction should make their intention clear, establish their voice as a credible one, and encourage a person to continue reading.

Conclusions tend to follow a similar pattern. In them, the writer restates their main idea a final time, often after summarizing the smaller pieces of that idea. If the introduction uses a quote or anecdote to grab the reader's attention, the conclusion often makes reference to it again. Whatever way the writer chooses to arrange the conclusion, the final restatement of the main idea should be clear and simple for the reader to interpret. Finally, conclusions shouldn't introduce any new information.

Organization

Depending on what the author is attempting to accomplish, certain formats or text structures work better than others. For example, a sequence structure might work for narration but not for identifying similarities and differences between concepts. Similarly, a comparison-contrast structure is not useful for narration. It's the author's job to put the right information in the correct format.

Readers should be familiar with the five main literary structures:

1. **Sequence** structure (sometimes referred to as the order structure) is when the order of events proceed in a predictable order. In many cases, this means the text goes through the plot elements: exposition, rising action, climax, falling action, and resolution. Readers are introduced to characters, setting, and conflict in the exposition. In the rising action, there's an increase in tension and suspense. The climax is the height of tension and the point of no return. Tension decreases during the falling action. In the resolution, any conflicts presented in the exposition are solved, and the story concludes. An informative text that is structured sequentially will often go in order from one step to the next.

2. In the **problem-solution** structure, authors identify a potential problem and suggest a solution. This form of writing is usually divided into two paragraphs and can be found in informational texts. For example, cell phone, cable, and satellite providers use this structure in manuals to help customers troubleshoot or identify problems with services or products.

3. When authors want to discuss similarities and differences between separate concepts, they arrange thoughts in a **comparison-contrast** paragraph structure. Venn diagrams are an effective graphic organizer for comparison-contrast structures because they feature two overlapping circles that can be used to organize similarities and differences. A comparison-contrast essay organizes one paragraph based on similarities and another based on differences. A comparison-contrast essay can also be arranged with the similarities and differences of individual traits addressed within individual paragraphs. Words such as *however*, *but*, and *nevertheless* help signal a contrast in ideas.

4. **Descriptive** writing structure is designed to appeal to your senses. Much like an artist who constructs a painting, good descriptive writing builds an image in the reader's mind by appealing to the five senses: sight, hearing, taste, touch, and smell. However, overly descriptive writing can become tedious; whereas sparse descriptions can make settings and characters seem flat. Good authors strike a balance by applying descriptions only to passages, characters, and settings that are integral to the plot.

5. Passages that use the **cause and effect** structure are simply asking *why* by demonstrating some type of connection between ideas. Words such as *if, since, because, then, or consequently* indicate a cause-and-effect relationship. By switching the order of a complex sentence, the writer can rearrange the emphasis on different clauses. Saying, *If Sheryl is late, we'll miss the dance*, is different from saying *We'll miss the dance if Sheryl is late*. One emphasizes Sheryl's tardiness while the other emphasizes missing the dance. Paragraphs can also be arranged in a cause and effect format. Since the format—before and

after—is sequential, it is useful when authors wish to discuss the impact of choices. Researchers often apply this paragraph structure to the scientific method.

Point of View

Point of view is an important writing device to consider. In fiction writing, point of view refers to who tells the story or from whose perspective readers are observing the story. In non-fiction writing, the **point of view** refers to whether authors refer to themselves, their readers, or choose not to refer to either. Whether fiction or nonfiction, the author will carefully consider the impact the perspective will have on the purpose and main point of the writing.

A. First-person point of view: The story is told from the writer's perspective. In fiction, this would mean that the main character is also the narrator. First-person point of view is easily recognized by the use of personal pronouns such as *I, me, we, us, our, my,* and *myself*.

B. Third-person point of view: In a more formal essay, this would be an appropriate perspective because the focus should be on the subject matter, not the writer or the reader. Third-person point of view is recognized using the pronouns *he, she, they,* and *it*. In fiction writing, third-person point of view has a few variations.

C. Third-person limited point of view: Refers to a story told by a narrator who has access to the thoughts and feelings of just one character.

D. Third-person omniscient point of view: The narrator has access to the thoughts and feelings of all the characters.

Point of View	Pronouns Used
First person	I, me, we, us, our, my, myself
Second person	You, your, yourself
Third person	He, she, it, they

E. Third-person objective point of view: The narrator is like a fly on the wall and can see and hear what the characters do and say but does not have access to their thoughts and feelings.

F. Second-person point of view: This point of view isn't commonly used in fiction or nonfiction writing because it directly addresses the reader using the pronouns *you, your,* and *yourself*. Second-person perspective is more appropriate in direct communication, such as business letters or emails.

How the Position and Purpose Shape the Text

Readers should always identify the author's position or stance in a text. No matter how objective a piece may seem, assume the author has preconceived beliefs. Reduce the likelihood of accepting an invalid argument by looking for multiple articles on the topic, including those with varying opinions. If several opinions point in the same direction, and are backed by reputable peer-reviewed sources, it's more likely the author has a valid argument. Positions that run contrary to widely held beliefs and existing data should invite scrutiny. There are exceptions to the rule, so be a careful consumer of information.

Though themes, symbols, and motifs are buried deep within the text and can sometimes be difficult to infer, an author's purpose is usually obvious from the beginning. There are four purposes of writing: to inform, to persuade, to describe, and to entertain. Informative writings present facts in an accessible way and are also known as expository writing. Persuasive writing appeals to emotions and logic to inspire the reader to adopt a specific stance. Be wary of this type of writing, as it often lacks objectivity. Descriptive writing is designed to paint a picture in the reader's mind, while texts that entertain are often narratives designed to engage and delight the reader.

The various writing styles are usually blended, with one purpose dominating the rest. For example, a persuasive piece might begin with a humorous tale to make readers more receptive to the persuasive message, or a recipe in a cookbook designed to inform might be preceded by an entertaining anecdote that makes the recipe more appealing.

Determining an Author's Point of View

A **rhetorical strategy**—also referred to as a **rhetorical mode**—is the structural way an author chooses to present their argument. Though the terms noted below are similar to the organizational structures noted earlier, these strategies do not imply that the entire text follows the approach. For example, a cause and effect organizational structure is solely that, nothing more. A persuasive text may use cause and effect as a strategy to convey a singular point. Thus, an argument may include several of the strategies as the author strives to convince their audience to take action or accept a different point of view. It's important that readers are able to identify an author's thesis and position on the topic in order to be able to identify the careful construction through which the author speaks to the reader. The following are some of the more common rhetorical strategies:

- **Cause and effect** — establishing a logical correlation or causation between two ideas
- **Classification/division** — the grouping of similar items together or division of something into parts
- **Comparison/contrast** — the distinguishing of similarities/differences to expand on an idea
- **Definition** — used to clarify abstract ideas, unfamiliar concepts, or to distinguish one idea from another
- **Description** — use of vivid imagery, active verbs, and clear adjectives to explain ideas
- **Exemplification** — the use of examples to explain an idea
- **Narration** — anecdotes or personal experience to present or expand on a concept
- **Problem/solution** — presentation of a problem or problems, followed by proposed solution(s)

Identifying Rhetorical Devices

If a writer feels strongly about a subject, or has a passion for it, strong words and phrases can be chosen. Think of the types of rhetoric (or language) our politicians use. Each word, phrase, and idea is carefully crafted to elicit a response. Hopefully, that response is one of agreement to a certain point of view, especially among voters. Authors use the same types of language to achieve the same results. For example, the word "bad" has a certain connotation, but the words "horrid," "repugnant," and "abhorrent" paint a far better picture for the reader. They're more precise. They're interesting to read and they should all illicit stronger feelings in the reader than the word "bad." An author generally uses other devices beyond mere word choice to persuade, convince, entertain, or otherwise engage a reader.

Rhetorical devices are those elements an author utilizes in painting sensory, and hopefully persuasive ideas to which a reader can relate. They are numerable. Test takers will likely encounter one or more standardized test questions addressing various rhetorical devices. This study guide will address the more common types: alliteration, irony, metaphor, simile, hyperbole, allegory, imagery, onomatopoeia, and personification, providing examples of each.

Alliteration is a device that uses repetitive beginning sounds in words to appeal to the reader. Classic tongue twisters are a great example of alliteration. *She sells sea shells down by the sea shore* is an extreme example of alliteration. Authors will use alliterative devices to capture a reader's attention. It's interesting to note that marketing also utilizes alliteration in the same way. A reader will likely remember products that have the brand name and item starting with the same letter. Similarly, many songs, poems, and catchy phrases use this device. It's memorable. Use of alliteration draws a reader's attention to ideas that an author wants to highlight.

Irony is a device that authors use when pitting two contrasting items or ideas against each other in order to create an effect. It's frequently used when an author wants to employ humor or convey a sarcastic tone. Additionally, it's often used in fictional works to build tension between characters, or between a particular character and the reader. An author may use *verbal irony* (sarcasm), *situational irony* (where actions or events have the opposite effect than what's expected), and *dramatic irony* (where the reader knows something a character does not). Examples of irony include:

Dramatic Irony: An author describing the presence of a hidden killer in a murder mystery, unbeknownst to the characters but known to the reader.

Situational Irony: An author relating the tale of a fire captain who loses her home in a five-alarm conflagration.

Verbal Irony: This is where an author or character says one thing but means another. For example, telling a police officer "Thanks a lot" after receiving a ticket.

Metaphor is a device that uses a figure of speech to paint a visual picture of something that is not literally applicable. Authors relate strong images to readers, and evoke similar strong feelings using metaphors. Most often, authors will mention one thing in comparison to another more familiar to the reader. It's important to note that metaphors do not use the comparative words "like" or "as." At times, metaphors encompass common phrases such as clichés. At other times, authors may use mixed metaphors in making identification between two dissimilar things. Examples of metaphors include:

- An author describing a character's anger as *a flaming sheet of fire.*
- An author relating a politician as having been a folding chair under close questioning.
- A novel's character telling another character to *take a flying hike.*
- Shakespeare's assertion that *all the world's a stage.*

Simile is a device that compares two dissimilar things using the words "like" and "as." When using similes, an author tries to catch a reader's attention and use comparison of unlike items to make a point. Similes are commonly used and often develop into figures of speech and catch phrases.

Examples of similes include:

- An author describing a character as having a complexion like a faded lily.
- An investigative journalist describing his interview subject as being like cold steel and with a demeanor hard as ice.
- An author asserting the current political arena is just like a three-ring circus and as dry as day old bread.

Similes and metaphors can be confusing. When utilizing simile, an author will state one thing is like another. A metaphor states one thing is another. An example of the difference would be if an author states a character is *just like a fierce tiger and twice as angry,* as opposed to stating the character *is a fierce tiger and twice as angry.*

Hyperbole is simply an exaggeration that is not taken literally. A potential test taker will have heard or employed hyperbole in daily speech, as it is a common device we all use. Authors will use hyperbole to draw a reader's eye toward important points and to illicit strong emotional and relatable responses. Examples of hyperbole include:

- An author describing a character as being as big as a house and twice the circumference of a city block.
- An author stating the city's water problem as being old as the hills and more expensive than a king's ransom in spent tax dollars.
- A journalist stating the mayoral candidate died of embarrassment when her tax records were made public.

Allegories are stories or poems with hidden meanings, usually a political or moral one. Authors will frequently use allegory when leading the reader to a conclusion. Allegories are similar to parables, symbols, and analogies. Often, an author will employ the use of allegory to make political, historical, moral, or social observations. As an example, Jonathan Swift's work *Gulliver's Travels into Several Remote Nations of the World* is an allegory in and of itself. The work is a political allegory of England during Jonathan Swift's lifetime. Set in the travel journal style plot of a giant amongst smaller people, and a smaller Gulliver amongst the larger, it is a commentary on Swift's political stance of existing issues of his age. Many fictional works are entire allegories in and of themselves. George Orwell's *Animal Farm* is a story of animals that conquer man and form their own farm society with swine at the top; however, it is not a literal story in any sense. It's Orwell's political allegory of Russian society during and after the Communist revolution of 1917. Other examples of allegory in popular culture include:

- Aesop's fable "The Tortoise and the Hare," which teaches readers that being steady is more important than being fast and impulsive.
- The popular *Hunger Games* by Suzanne Collins that teaches readers that media can numb society to what is truly real and important.
- Dr. Seuss's *Yertle the Turtle* which is a warning against totalitarianism and, at the time it was written, against the despotic rule of Adolf Hitler.

Imagery is a rhetorical device that an author employs when they use visual or descriptive language to evoke a reader's emotion. Use of imagery as a rhetorical device is broader in scope than this study guide addresses, but in general, the function of imagery is to create a vibrant scene in the reader's imagination and, in turn, tease the reader's ability to identify through strong emotion and sensory experience. In the simplest of terms, imagery, as a rhetoric device, beautifies literature.

An example of poetic imagery is below:

> Pain has an element of blank
>
> It cannot recollect
>
> When it began, or if there were
>
> A day when it was not.
>
> It has no future but itself,
>
> Its infinite realms contain
>
> Its past, enlightened to perceive
>
> New periods of pain.

In the above poem, Emily Dickenson uses strong imagery. Pain is equivalent to an "element of blank" or of nothingness. Pain cannot recollect a beginning or end, as if it was a person (see *personification* below). Dickenson appeals to the reader's sense of a painful experience by discussing the unlikelihood that discomfort sees a future, but does visualize a past and present. She simply indicates that pain, through the use of imagery, is cyclical and never ending. Dickenson's theme is one of painful depression, and it is through the use of imagery that she conveys this to her readers.

Onomatopoeia is the author's use of words that create sound. Words like *pop* and *sizzle* are examples of onomatopoeia. When an author wants to draw a reader's attention in an auditory sense, they will use onomatopoeia. An author may also use onomatopoeia to create sounds as interjection or commentary. Examples include:

- An author describing a cat's vocalization as the kitten's chirrup echoed throughout the empty cabin.
- A description of a campfire as crackling and whining against its burning green wood.
- An author relating the sound of a car accident as metallic screeching against crunching asphalt.
- A description of an animal roadblock as being a symphonic melody of groans, baas, and moans.

Personification is a rhetorical device that an author uses to attribute human qualities to inanimate objects or animals. Once again, this device is useful when an author wants the reader to strongly relate to an idea. As in the example of George Orwell's *Animal Farm*, many of the animals are given the human abilities to speak, reason, apply logic, and otherwise interact as humans do. This helps the reader see how easily it is for any society to segregate into the haves and the have-nots through the manipulation of power. Personification is a device that enables the reader to empathize through human experience.

Examples of personification include:

- An author describing the wind as *whispering through the trees*.
- A description of a stone wall as being a hardened, unmovable creature made of cement and brick.
- An author attributing a city building as having slit eyes and an unapproachable, foreboding façade.
- An author describing spring as a beautiful bride, blooming in white, ready for summer's matrimony.

When identifying rhetorical devices, look for words and phrases that capture one's attention. Make note of the author's use of comparison between the inanimate and the animate. Consider words that make the reader feel sounds and envision imagery. Pay attention to the rhythm of fluid sentences and to the use of words that evoke emotion. The ability to identify rhetorical devices is another step in achieving successful reading comprehension and in being able to correctly answer standardized questions related to those devices.

Understanding Methods Used to Appeal to a Specific Audience

In an argument or persuasive text, an author will strive to sway readers to an opinion or conclusion. To be effective, an author must consider their intended audience. Although an author may write text for a general audience, he or she will use methods of appeal or persuasion to convince that audience. Aristotle asserted that there were three methods or modes by which a person could be persuaded. These are referred to as **rhetorical appeals**.

The three main types of rhetorical appeals are shown in the following graphic.

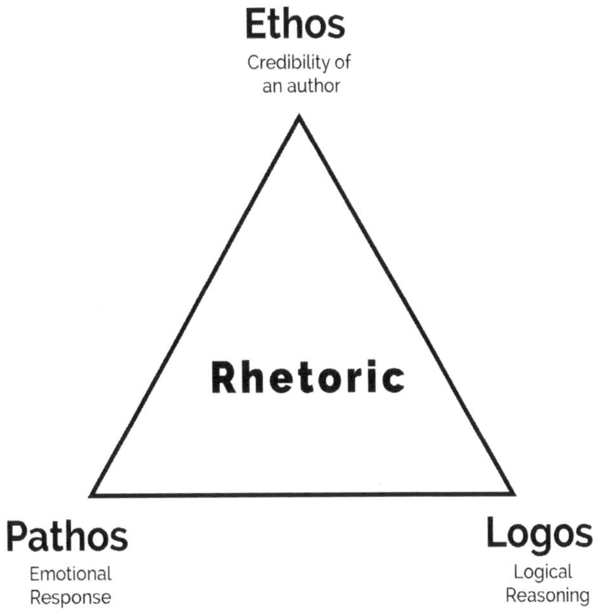

Ethos, also referred to as an **ethical appeal**, is an appeal to the audience's perception of the writer as credible (or not), based on their examination of their ethics and who the writer is, their experience or incorporation of relevant information, or their argument. For example, authors may present testimonials to bolster their arguments. The reader who critically examines the veracity of the testimonials and the credibility of those giving the testimony will be able to determine if the author's use of testimony is valid to their argument. In turn, this will help the reader determine if the author's thesis is valid. An author's careful and appropriate use of technical language can create an overall knowledgeable effect and, in turn, act as a convincing vehicle when it comes to credibility. Overuse of technical language, however, may create confusion in readers and obscure an author's overall intent.

Pathos, also referred to as **emotional appeal**, is an appeal to the audience's sense of identity, self-interest, or emotions. A critical reader will notice when the author is appealing to pathos through anecdotes and descriptions that elicit an emotion such as anger or pity. Readers should also beware of factual information that uses generalization to appeal to the emotions. While it's tempting to believe an author is the source of truth in their text, an author who presents factual information as universally true, consistent throughout time, and common to all groups is using **generalization**. Authors who exclusively use generalizations without specific facts and credible sourcing are attempting to sway readers solely through emotion.

Logos, also referred to as a **logical appeal**, is an appeal to the audience's ability to see and understand the logic in a claim offered by the writer. A critical reader has to be able to evaluate an author's arguments for validity of reasoning and for sufficiency when it comes to argument.

Synthesis

Synthesis in reading involves the ability to fully comprehend text passages, and then going further by making new connections to see things in a new or different way. It involves a full thought process and requires readers to change the way they think about what they read.

Synthesis goes further than summary. When **summarizing**, a reader collects all of the information an author presents in a text passage, and restates it in an effective manner. Synthesis requires that the test taker not only summarize reading material, but be able to express new ideas based on the author's message. It is a full culmination of all reading comprehension strategies. It will require the test taker to order, recount, summarize, and recreate information into a whole new idea.

In utilizing synthesis, a reader must be able to form mental images about what they read, recall any background information they have about the topic, ask critical questions about the material, determine the importance of points an author makes, make inferences based on the reading, and finally be able to form new ideas based on all of the above skills. Synthesis requires the reader to make connections, visualize concepts, determine their importance, ask questions, make inferences, then fully synthesize all of this information into new thought.

Making Connections in Reading

There are three helpful thinking strategies to keep in mind when attempting to synthesize text passages:

- Think about how the content of a passage relates to life experience.
- Think about how the content of a passage relates to other text.
- Think about how the content of a passage relates to the world in general.

When reading a given passage, the test taker should actively think about how the content relates to their life experience. While the author's message may express an opinion different from what the reader believes, or express ideas with which the reader is unfamiliar, a good reader will try to relate any of the author's details to their own familiar ground. A reader should use context clues to understand unfamiliar terminology, and recognize familiar information they have encountered in prior experience. Bringing prior life experience and knowledge to the test-taking situation is helpful in making connections. The ability to relate an unfamiliar idea to something the reader already knows is critical in understanding unique and new ideas.

When trying to make connections while reading, keep the following questions in mind:

- How does this feel familiar in personal experience?
- How is this similar to or different from other reading?
- How is this familiar in the real world?
- How does this relate to the world in general?

A reader should ask themself these questions during the act of reading in order to actively make connections to past and present experiences. Utilizing the ability to make connections is an important step in achieving synthesis.

Determining Importance in Reading

Being able to determine what is most important while reading is critical to synthesis. It is the difference between being able to tell what is necessary to full comprehension and that which is interesting but not necessary.

When determining the importance of an author's ideas, consider the following:

- Ask how critical an author's particular idea, assertion, or concept is to the overall message.
- Ask "is this an interesting fact or is this information essential to understanding the author's main idea?"
- Make a simple chart. On one side, list all of the important, essential points an author makes and on the other, list all of the interesting yet non-critical ideas.
- Highlight, circle, or underline any dates or data in non-fiction passages. Pay attention to headings, captions, and any graphs or diagrams.
- When reading a fictional passage, delineate important information such as theme, character, setting, conflict (what the problem is), and resolution (how the problem is fixed). Most often, these are the most important aspects contained in fictional text.
- If a non-fiction passage is instructional in nature, take physical note of any steps in the order of their importance as presented by the author. Look for words such as *first*, *next*, *then*, and *last*.

Determining the importance of an author's ideas is critical to synthesis in that it requires the test taker to parse out any unnecessary information and demonstrate they have the ability to make sound determination on what is important to the author, and what is merely a supporting or less critical detail.

Asking Questions While Reading

A reader must ask questions while reading. This demonstrates their ability to critically approach information and apply higher thinking skills to an author's content. Some of these questions have been addressed earlier in this section. A reader must ask what is or isn't important, what relates to their experience, and what relates to the world in general. However, it's important to ask other questions as well in order to make connections and synthesize reading material.

Consider the following partial list of possibilities:

- What type of passage is this? Is it fiction? Non-fiction? Does it include data?
- Based on the type of passage, what information should be noted in order to make connections, visualize details, and determine importance?
- What is the author's message or theme? What is it they want the reader to understand?
- Is this passage trying to convince readers of something? What is it? If so, is the argument logical, convincing, and effective? How so? If not, how not?
- What do readers already know about this topic? Are there other viewpoints that support or contradict it?
- Is the information in this passage current and up to date?
- Is the author trying to teach readers a lesson? If so, what is it? Is there a moral to this story?
- How does this passage relate to experience?
- What is not as understandable in this passage? What context clues can help with understanding?
- What conclusions can be drawn? What predictions can be made?

Again, the above should be considered only a small example of the possibilities. Any question the reader asks while reading will help achieve synthesis and full reading comprehension.

Connections Between Different Texts

When analyzing two or more texts, there are several different aspects that need to be considered, particularly the styles (or the artful way in which the authors use diction to deliver a theme), points of view, and types of argument. In order to do so, one should compare and contrast the following elements between the texts:

- **Style**: narrative, persuasive, descriptive, informative, etc.
- **Tone**: sarcastic, angry, somber, humorous, etc.
- **Sentence structure**: simple (1 clause) compound (2 clauses), complex-compound (3 clauses)
- **Punctuation choice**: question marks, exclamation points, periods, dashes, etc.
- **Point of view**: first person, second person, third person
- **Paragraph structure**: long, short, both, differences between the two
- **Organizational structure**: compare/contrast, problem/solution, chronological, etc.

The following two poems and the essay concern the theme of death and are presented to demonstrate how to evaluate the above elements:

Poem 1:

How wonderful is Death,

Death, and his brother Sleep!

One, pale as yonder waning moon

With lips of lurid blue;

The other, rosy as the morn

When throned on ocean's wave

It blushes o'er the world;

Yet both so passing wonderful!

"Queen Mab," Percy Bysshe Shelley

Poem 2:

After great pain, a formal feeling comes –

The Nerves sit ceremonious, like Tombs –

The stiff Heart questions 'was it He, that bore,'

And 'Yesterday, or Centuries before'?

The Feet, mechanical, go round –

A Wooden way

Of Ground, or Air, or Ought –

Regardless grown,

A Quartz contentment, like a stone –

This is the Hour of Lead –

Remembered, if outlived,

As Freezing persons, recollect the Snow –

First – Chill – then Stupor – then the letting go –

"After Great Pain, A Formal Feeling Comes," Emily Dickinson

Essay 1

The Process of Dying

Death occurs in several stages. The first stage is the pre-active stage, which occurs a few days to weeks before death, in which the desire to eat and drink decreases, and the person may feel restless, irritable, and anxious. The second stage is the active stage, where the skin begins to cool, breathing becomes difficult as the lungs become congested (known as the "death rattle"), and the person loses control of their bodily fluids.

Once death occurs, there are also two stages. The first is clinical death, when the heart stops pumping blood and breathing ceases. This stage lasts approximately 4-6 minutes, and during this time, it is possible for a victim to be resuscitated via CPR or a defibrillator. After 6 minutes however, the oxygen stores within the brain begin to deplete, and the victim enters biological death. This is the point of no return, as the cells of the brain and vital organs begin to die, a process that is irreversible.

Now, using the outline above, the similarities and differences between the two passages are considered:

1. **Style**: The two poems are both descriptive as they focus on descriptions and sensations to convey their messages and do not follow any sort of timeline. The third selection is an expository style, presenting purely factual evidence on death, completely devoid of emotion.

2. **Tone**: Readers should notice the differences in the word choices between the two poems. Percy Shelley's word choices—"wonderful," "rosy," "blushes," "ocean"—surrounding death indicates that he views death in a welcoming manner as his words carry positive charges. The word choices by Dickinson, however, carry negative connotations—"pain," "wooden," "stone," "lead," "chill," "tombs"—which indicates an aversion to death. In contrast, the expository passage has no emotionally-charged words of any kind and seems to view death simply as a process that happens, neither welcoming nor fearing it. The tone in this passage, therefore, is neutral.

3. **Sentence structure**: Shelley's poem is composed mostly of compound sentences, which flow easily into one another. If read aloud, it sounds almost fluid, like the waves of the ocean he describes in his poem. His sentence structure mirrors the ease in which he views death. Dickinson's poem, on the other hand, is mostly simple sentences that are short and curt. They do not flow easily into one another, possibly representing her hesitancy and discomfort in her views of death. The expository passage contains many complex-compound sentences, which are used to accommodate lots of information. The structure of these sentences contributes to the overall informative nature of the selection.

4. **Punctuation choice**: Shelley uses commas, semicolons, and exclamation points in his poem, which, combined with his word choices and sentence structure, contributes to the overall positive tone of the poem. Dickinson uses lots of dashes, which make the poem feel almost cutting and jagged, which contributes to the overall negative tone of her poem. The expository text uses only commas and periods, which adds to the overall neutral tone of the selection.

5. **Point of view**: The point of view in all three selections is third person. In the two poems, there are no obvious pronouns; however, they both are presented in the third-person point of view, as Shelley speaks of Death in the third person, and Dickinson refers to "freezing persons." Generally, if there

are no first- or second-person pronouns in a selection, the view is third person. The informational selection also uses third-person point of view, as it avoids any first- or second-person pronouns.

6. **Paragraph/stanza structure**: Shelley's poem is one stanza long, making it inherently simple in nature. The simplicity of the single stanza is representative (again) of the comfort in which the author finds the topic of death. Dickinson's poem is much lengthier, and comparatively, could signify the difficulty of letting go of the death of a loved one. The paragraph structure of the essay is much longer than the two and is used to fit in a lot more information than the poems, as the poems are trying to convey emotion, and the essay is presenting facts.

7. **Organizational structure**: Shelley's poem uses a compare and contrast method to illustrate the similarities between death and sleep: that death is merely a paler, bluer brother to the warm and rosy sleep. Dickinson's structure, however, is descriptive, focusing primarily on feelings and sensations. The expository passage, on the other hand, is chronologically-organized, as it follows a timeline of events that occur in stages.

When analyzing the different structures, it may be helpful to make a table and use single words to compare and contrast the texts:

Elements	**Queen Mab**	**After Great Pain**	**Process of Dying**
Style	Descriptive	Descriptive	Expository
Tone	Warm	Cold	Neutral
Sentence Structure	Fluid	Jagged	Long
Punctuation Choice	!	–	.
Point of View	Third	Third	Third
Paragraph Structure	Short	Longer	Longest
Organizational Structure	Compare-Contrast	Descriptive	Chronological

Using this table, the differences become very clear. Although the two poems are both about death, their word tone, sentence structure, punctuation choices, and organization depict differences in how the authors perceive death, while the elements in the expository text clearly indicate an objective view of death. It should be noted that these are only a handful of the endless possible interpretations the reader could make.

Vocabulary

Identifying Roots

By analyzing and understanding Latin, Greek, and Anglo-Saxon word roots and structure, authors better convey the thoughts they want to express to the readers of their words and help them to determine their meanings within the flow and without their missing a beat. For instance, **context**—how words are used in sentences—is from the Latin for *contextus*, which means "together" + "to weave," and gives readers a graphic for the minds' eyes to see the coming together of their usage. Like every other topic discussed herein, context is needed for understanding. This element actually has a second, crucial meaning. Context is not only the *how*, but the revealed moment of the *why* a writing has been composed; it is the "Aha" moment.

The way *how* words are used in sentences is important because it also gives meaning and cohesion from sentence to sentence, paragraph to paragraph, and page after page. In other words, it gives the document continuity.

Another upside of the how side is that readers have opportunities to understand new words with which they are unfamiliar. Of course, people can always look words up if a dictionary or thesaurus, if available, but meaning might be gleaned on the spot in a piece that is well-written. **Synonyms** (words or phrases that mean about the same) and **antonyms** (words or phrases that mean the opposite of the specific word) in context give clues to meanings, and sometimes reiteration of a word might add clarification. Repetition, wisely used, can also serve as a part of how a piece flows.

The revealed moment of the *why* is important because context, up to that moment, has determined the shape of the text. This is, essentially, to bring out what it is all about.

Prefixes

A **prefix** is a word, letter, or number that is placed before another. It adjusts or qualifies the original word's meaning.

Four prefixes represent 97 percent of English words with prefixes. They are:

- *dis-* means "not" or "opposite of"; *dis*abled
- in-, im-, il-, ir- mean "not"; illiterate
- *re-* means "again"; *re*turn
- *un-* means "not"; *un*predictable
- Other commons prefixes include:
- *anti-* means "against"; antibacterial
- *fore-* means "before"; forefront
- *mis-* means "wrongly"; misunderstand
- *non-* means "not"; nonsense
- *over-* means "over"; overabundance
- *pre-* means "before"; preheat
- *super-* means "above"; superman

Suffixes

The official definition of a **suffix** is "a morpheme added at the end of a word to form a derivative." In English, that means a suffix is a letter or group of letters added at the end of a word to form another word. The word created with the addition is either a different tense of the same word (*help + ed = helped)* or a new word (*help + ful = helpful)*.

They are:

- *-ed* is used to make present tense verbs into past tense verbs; wash*ed*
- *-ing* is used to make a present tense verb into a present participle verb; wash*ing*
- *-ly* is used to make characteristic of; love*ly*
- *-s* or *–es* are used to make more than one; chair*s* or box*es*
- Other common suffixes include:
- *-able* means can be done; deplor*able*
- *-al* means having characteristics of; comic*al*
- *-est* means comparative; great*est*
- *-ful* means full of; wonder*ful*
- *-ism* means belief in; commun*ism*
- *-less* means without; faith*less*
- *-ment* means action or process; accomplish*ment*
- *-ness* means state of; happ*iness*
- *-ize* means to render, to make; terror*ize,* steril*ize*
- *-ise* is primarily the British variant of *–ize;* surpr*ise,* advert*ise*
- -ced means go; spelling variations include -cede (concede, recede); -ceed (only three: proceed, exceed, succeed); -sede (the only one: supersede)

(Note: In some of the examples above, the *e* has been deleted.)

Finding the Meaning of Words and Phrases in Context

There will be many occasions in one's reading career in which an unknown word or a word with multiple meanings will pop up. There are ways of determining what these words or phrases mean that do not require the use of the dictionary, which is especially helpful during a test where one may not be available. Even outside of the exam, knowing how to derive an understanding of a word via **context clues** will be a critical skill in the real world. The context is the circumstances in which a story or a passage is happening, and can usually be found in the series of words directly before or directly after the word or phrase in question. The clues are the words that hint towards the meaning of the unknown word or phrase. The author may use synonyms or antonyms that you can use. **Synonyms** refer to words that have the same meaning as another word (e.g., instructor/teacher/educator, canine/dog, feline/cat, herbivore/vegetarian). **Antonyms** refer to words that have the opposite meaning as another word (e.g., true/false, up/down, in/out, right/wrong).

There may be questions that ask about the meaning of a particular word or phrase within a passage. There are a couple ways to approach these kinds of questions:

- Define the word or phrase in a way that is easy to comprehend (using context clues).
- Try out each answer choice in place of the word.

To demonstrate, here's an example from *Alice in Wonderland*:

> Alice was beginning to get very tired of sitting by her sister on the bank, and of having nothing to do: once or twice she peeped into the book her sister was reading, but it had no pictures or conversations in it, "and what is the use of a book," thought Alice, "without pictures or conversations?"

Q: As it is used in the selection, the word peeped means:

Using the first technique, before looking at the answers, define the word "peeped" using context clues and then find the matching answer. Then, analyze the entire passage in order to determine the meaning, not just the surrounding words.

To begin, imagine a blank where the word should be and put a synonym or definition there: "once or twice she ___ into the book her sister was reading." The context clue here is the book. It may be tempting to put "read" where the blank is, but notice the preposition word, "into." One does not read *into* a book, one simply reads a book, and since reading a book requires that it is seen with a pair of eyes, then "look" would make the most sense to put into the blank: "once or twice she looked into the book her sister was reading."

Once an easy-to-understand word or synonym has been supplanted, check to make sure it makes sense with the rest of the passage. What happened after she looked into the book? She thought to herself how a book without pictures or conversations is useless. This situation in its entirety makes sense.

Now check the answer choices for a match:

a. To make a high-pitched cry
b. To smack
c. To look curiously
d. To pout

Since the word was already defined, answer choice (c) is the best option.

Using the second technique, replace the figurative blank with each of the answer choices and determine which one is the most appropriate. Remember to look further into the passage to clarify that they work, because they could still make sense out of context.

Once or twice she made a high pitched cry into the book her sister was reading.

Once or twice she smacked the book her sister was reading.

Once or twice she looked curiously into the book her sister was reading.

Once or twice she pouted into the book her sister was reading.

For Choice *A*, it does not make much sense in any context for a person to yell into a book, unless maybe something terrible has happened in the story. Given that afterward Alice thinks to herself how useless a book without pictures is, this option does not make sense within context.

For Choice *B*, smacking a book someone is reading may make sense if the rest of the passage indicates there a reason for doing so. If Alice was angry or her sister had shoved it in her face, then maybe smacking the book would make sense within context. However, since whatever she does with the book causes her to think, "what is the use of a book without pictures or conversations?" then answer Choice *B* is not an appropriate answer.

Answer Choice *C* fits well within context, given her subsequent thoughts on the matter.

Answer Choice *D* does not make sense in context or grammatically, as people do not "pout into" things.

This is a simple example to illustrate the techniques outlined above. There may, however, be a question in which all of the definitions are correct and also make sense out of context, in which the appropriate context clues will really need to be honed in on in order to determine the correct answer. For example, here is another passage from *Alice in Wonderland*:

> ... but when the Rabbit actually took a watch out of its waistcoat pocket, and looked at it, and then hurried on, Alice started to her feet, for it flashed across her mind that she had never before seen a rabbit with either a waistcoat-pocket or a watch to take out of it, and burning with curiosity, she ran across the field after it, and was just in time to see it pop down a large rabbit-hole under the hedge.

Q: As it is used in the passage, the word started means:

a. To turn on
b. To begin
c. To move quickly
d. To be surprised

All of these words qualify as a definition of start, but using context clues, the correct answer can be identified using one of the two techniques above. It's easy to see that one does not turn on, begin, or be surprised to one's feet. The selection also states that she "ran across the field after it," indicating that she was in a hurry. Therefore, to move quickly would make the most sense in this context.

The same strategies can be applied to vocabulary that may be completely unfamiliar. In this case, focus on the words before or after the unknown word in order to determine its definition. Take this sentence, for example:

"Sam was such a miser that he forced Andrew to pay him twelve cents for the candy, even though he had a large inheritance and he knew his friend was poor."

Unlike with assertion questions, for vocabulary questions, it may be necessary to apply some critical thinking skills that may not be explicitly stated within the passage. Think about the implications of the passage, or what the text is trying to say. With this example, it is important to realize that it is considered unusually stingy for a person to demand so little money from someone instead of just letting their friend have the candy, especially if this person is already wealthy. Hence, a miser is a greedy or stingy individual.

Questions about complex vocabulary may not be explicitly asked, but this is a useful skill to know. If there is an unfamiliar word while reading a passage and its definition goes unknown, it is possible to miss out on a critical message that could inhibit the ability to appropriately answer the questions. Practicing this technique in daily life will sharpen this ability to derive meanings from context clues with ease.

Practice Quiz

Questions 1-5 are based upon the following passage:

The Myth of Head Heat Loss

It has recently been brought to my attention that most people believe that 75% of your body heat is lost through your head. I had certainly heard this before, and am not going to attempt to say I didn't believe it when I first heard it. It is natural to be gullible to anything said with enough authority. But the "fact" that the majority of your body heat is lost through your head is a lie.

Let me explain. Heat loss is proportional to surface area exposed. An elephant loses a great deal more heat than an anteater because it has a much greater surface area than an anteater. Each cell has mitochondria that produce energy in the form of heat, and it takes a lot more energy to run an elephant than an anteater.

So, each part of your body loses its proportional amount of heat in accordance with its surface area. The human torso probably loses the most heat, though the legs lose a significant amount as well. Some people have asked, "Why does it feel so much warmer when you cover your head than when you don't?" Well, that's because your head, because it is not clothed, is losing a lot of heat while the clothing on the rest of your body provides insulation. If you went outside with a hat and pants but no shirt, not only would you look stupid but your heat loss would be significantly greater because so much more of you would be exposed. So, if given the choice to cover your chest or your head in the cold, choose the chest. It could save your life.

1. What is the primary purpose of this passage?
    a. To provide evidence that disproves a myth
    b. To compare elephants and anteaters
    c. To explain why it is appropriate to wear clothes in winter
    d. To show how people are gullible

2. Which of the following best describes the main idea of the passage?
    a. It is better to wear a shirt than a hat
    b. Heat loss is proportional to surface area exposed
    c. It is natural to be gullible
    d. The human chest loses the most heat

3. Why does the author compare elephants and anteaters?
    a. To express an opinion
    b. To give an example that helps clarify the main point
    c. To show the differences between them
    d. To persuade why one is better than the other

4. Which of the following best describes the tone of the passage?
    a. Harsh
    b. Angry
    c. Casual
    d. Indifferent

5. Which of the following sentences provides the best evidence to support the main idea?
   a. "It is natural to be gullible to anything said with enough authority."
   b. "Each part of your body loses its proportional amount of heat in accordance with its surface area."
   c. "If given the choice to cover your chest or your head in the cold, choose the chest."
   d. "But the 'fact' that the majority of your body heat is lost through your head is a lie.

See answers on next page.

Answer Explanations

1. A: Not only does the article provide examples to disprove a myth, the title also suggests that the article is trying to disprove a myth. Further, the sentence, "But the 'fact' that the majority of your body heat is lost through your head is a lie," and then the subsequent "let me explain," demonstrates the author's intention in disproving a myth. *B* is incorrect because although the selection does compare elephants and anteaters, it does so in order to prove a point, and is not the primary reason that the selection was written. *C* is incorrect because even though the article mentions somebody wearing clothes in the winter, and that doing so could save your life, wearing clothes in the winter is not the primary reason this article was written. *D* is incorrect because the article only mentions that people are gullible once, and makes no further comment on the matter, so this cannot be the primary purpose.

2. B: If the myth is that most of one's body heat is lost through their head, then the fact that heat loss is proportional to surface area exposed is the best evidence that disproves it, since one's head is a great deal less surface area than the rest of the body, making *B* the correct choice. "It is better to wear a shirt than a hat" does not provide evidence that disproves the fact that the head loses more heat than the rest of the body. Thus, *A* is incorrect. *C* is incorrect because gullibility is mentioned only once in this passage and the rest of the article ignores this statement, so clearly it is not the main idea. Finally, *D* is incorrect because though the article mentions that the human chest probably loses the most heat, it is to provide an example of the evidence that heat loss is proportional to surface area exposed, so this is not the main idea of the passage.

3. B: Choice *B* is correct because the author is trying to demonstrate the main idea, which is that heat loss is proportional to surface area, and so they compare two animals with different surface areas to clarify the main point. Choice *A* is incorrect because the author uses elephants and anteaters to prove a point that heat loss is proportional to surface area, not to express an opinion. Choice *C* is incorrect because though the author does use them to show differences, they do so in order to give examples that prove the above points. Choice *D* is incorrect because there is no language to indicate favoritism between the two animals.

4. C: Because of the way the author addresses the reader and the colloquial language the author uses (i.e., "let me explain," "so," "well," didn't," "you would look stupid," etc.), Choice *C* is the best answer because it has a much more casual tone than the usual informative article. Choice *A* may be a tempting choice because the author says the "fact" that most of one's heat is lost through their head is a "lie" and that someone who does not wear a shirt in the cold looks stupid. However, this only happens twice within the passage, and the passage does not give an overall tone of harshness. Choice *B* is incorrect because again, while not necessarily nice, the language does not carry an angry charge. The author is clearly not indifferent to the subject because of the passionate language that they use, so Choice *D* is incorrect.

5. B: Choice *B* is correct. The primary purpose of the article is to provide evidence to disprove the myth that most of a person's heat is lost through their head. The fact that each part of the body loses heat in proportion to its surface area is the best evidence to disprove this myth. Choice *A* is incorrect because again, gullibility is not a main contributor to this article, but it may be common to see questions on the test that give the same wrong answer in order to try and trick the test taker. Choice *C* only suggests what you should do with this information; it is not the primary evidence itself. Choice *D,* while tempting, is actually not evidence. It does not give any reason for why it is a lie; it simply states that it is. Evidence is factual information that supports a claim.

Practice Test #1

Algebra and Functions

1. What is the solution for the following equation?

$$\frac{x^2 + x - 30}{x - 5} = 11$$

a. $x = -6$
b. There is no solution.
c. $x = 16$
d. $x = 5$

2. What is the slope of this line?

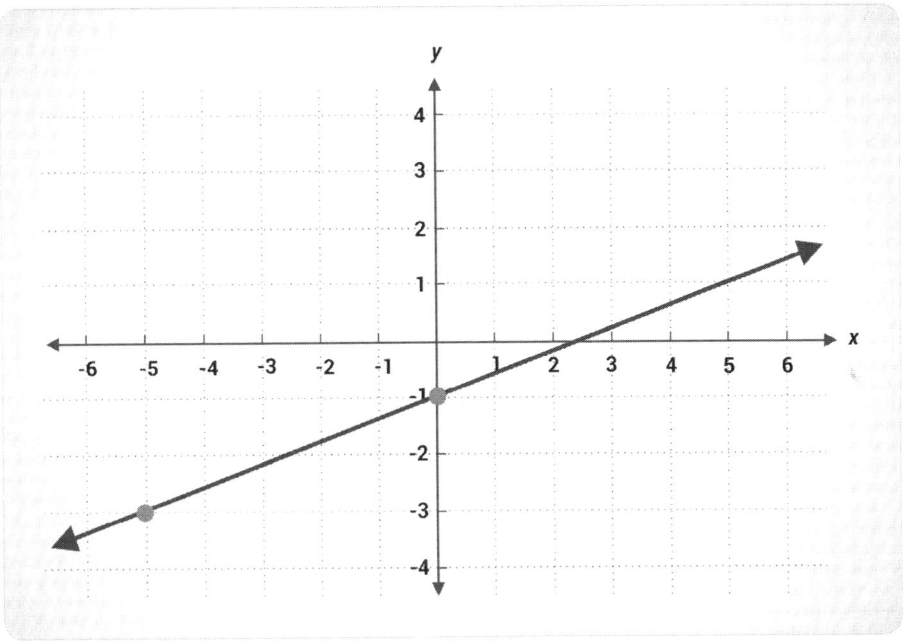

a. 2
b. $\frac{5}{2}$
c. $\frac{1}{2}$
d. $\frac{2}{5}$

3. Which of the following equations best represents the problem below?

The width of a rectangle is 2 centimeters less than the length. If the perimeter of the rectangle is 44 centimeters, then what are the dimensions of the rectangle?

a. $2l + 2(l - 2) = 44$
b. $(l + 2) + (l + 2) + l = 48$
c. $l \times (l - 2) = 44$
d. $(l + 2) + (l + 2) + l = 44$

4. The variable y is directly proportional to x. If $y = 3$ when $x = 5$, then what is y when $x = 20$?
   a. 10
   b. 12
   c. 14
   d. 16

5. If $-3(x + 4) \geq x + 8$, what is the value of x?
   a. $x = 4$
   b. $x \geq 2$
   c. $x \geq -5$
   d. $x \leq -5$

6. A rectangle has a length that is 5 feet longer than three times its width. If the perimeter is 90 feet, what is the length in feet?
   a. 10
   b. 20
   c. 25
   d. 35

7. An investment of $2,000 is made into an account with an annual interest rate of 5%, compounded continuously. What is the total value for the investment after eight years?
   a. $2,954.91
   b. $3,000
   c. $2,983.65
   d. $2,800

8. Ten students take a test. Five students get a 50. Four students get a 70. If the average score is 55, what was the last student's score?
   a. 20
   b. 40
   c. 50
   d. 60

9. Consider a cashier that averages 50 customers per hour. What is the probability in which the arrival time between customers is less than 1 minute?
   a. 57%
   b. 53%
   c. 100%
   d. 50%

10. What is the value of x in the following expression?

$$4x - 12 = -2x$$

   a. 2
   b. 3
   c. -6
   d. -2

11. What is the simplified quotient of the following expression?

$$\frac{5x^3}{3x^2y} \div \frac{25}{3y^9}$$

a. $\frac{125x}{9y^{10}}$
b. $\frac{x}{5y^8}$
c. $\frac{5}{xy^8}$
d. $\frac{xy^8}{5}$

12. The area of a given rectangle is 24 square centimeters. If the measure of each side is multiplied by 3, what is the area of the new figure?

a. 48 cm
b. 72 cm
c. 216 cm
d. 13,824 cm

13. If the ordered pair $(-3,-4)$ is reflected over the x-axis, what's the new ordered pair?

a. $(-3,-4)$
b. $(3,-4)$
c. $(3,4)$
d. $(-3,4)$

14. What would the equation be for the following problem?

3 times the sum of a number and 7 is greater than or equal to 32

a. $3(7n) > 32$
b. $3 \times n + 7 \geq 32$
c. $3n + 21 > 32$
d. $3(n + 7) \geq 32$

15. The table below shows tickets purchased during the week for entry to the local zoo. What is the mean of adult tickets sold for the week?

Day of the Week	**Age**	**Tickets Sold**
Monday	Adult	22
Monday	Child	30
Tuesday	Adult	16
Tuesday	Child	15
Wednesday	Adult	24
Wednesday	Child	23
Thursday	Adult	19
Thursday	Child	26
Friday	Adult	29
Friday	Child	38

a. 24.2
b. 21
c. 22
d. 26.4

16. Courtney leaves home and drives her truck 1,236 yards towards her destination. Her destination is 6,292 feet away from her home. How many more feet does she need to travel before she arrives?
a. 2,284
b. 3,708
c. 5,056
d. 2,584

17. Which inequality represents the number line below?

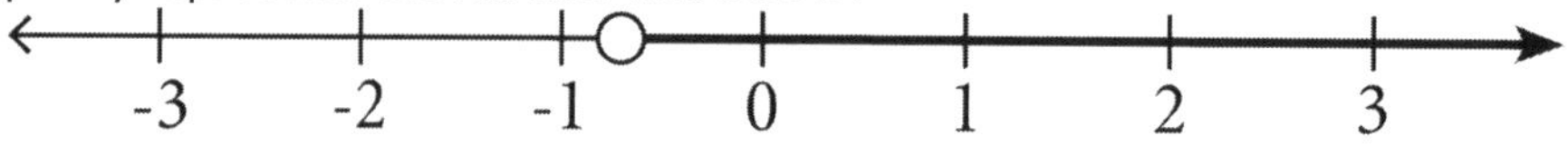

a. $4x + 5 < 8$
b. $-4x + 5 < 8$
c. $-4x + 5 > 8$
d. $4x - 5 > 8$

18. What is the slope of the line that passes through the points $(10, -4)$ and $(-5, 8)$?
a. $-\frac{5}{4}$
b. $-\frac{4}{15}$
c. $-\frac{4}{5}$
d. $-\frac{12}{5}$

19. Points L and M lie on line KN. The length of line KN is 30 units long, LN is 20 units long, and KM is 16 units long. How many units long is LM?

a. 16
b. 14
c. 10
d. 6

20. A data set is comprised of the following values: 30, 33, 33, 26, 27, 32, 33, 35, 29, 27. Which of the following has the greatest value?

a. Mean
b. Median
c. Mode
d. Range

21. A group of marathon runners were surveyed to see how many miles they ran in a week to prepare for the upcoming race. Six runners were surveyed, and the median of the responses was 14 miles. Which of the following is a possible list of responses?

a. 11, 12, 15, 16, 11, 13
b. 13, 16, 11, 12, 15, 16
c. 16, 16, 14, 13, 11, 12
d. 12, 15, 16, 13, 16, 15

22. What is the value of $x^2 - 2xy + 2y^2$ when $x = 2, y = 3$?

a. 8
b. 10
c. 12
d. 14

23. $(2x - 4y)^2 =$

a. $4x^2 - 16xy + 16y^2$
b. $4x^2 - 8xy + 16y^2$
c. $4x^2 - 16xy - 16y^2$
d. $2x^2 - 8xy + 8y^2$

24. If $x > 3$, then $\frac{x^2-6x+9}{x^2-x-6} =$

a. $\frac{x+2}{x-3}$
b. $\frac{x-2}{x-3}$
c. $\frac{x-3}{x+3}$
d. $\frac{x-3}{x+2}$

25. If $4x - 3 = 5$, what is the value of x?
    a. 1
    b. 2
    c. 3
    d. 4

26. What are the zeros of the function: $f(x) = x^3 + 4x^2 + 4x$?
    a. −2
    b. 0, −2
    c. 2
    d. 0, 2

27. If $g(x) = x^3 - 3x^2 - 2x + 6$ and $f(x) = 2$, then what is $g(f(x))$?
    a. −26
    b. 6
    c. $2x^3 - 6x^2 - 4x + 12$
    d. −2

28. What is the function that forms an equivalent graph to $y = \cos(x)$?
    a. $y = \tan(x)$
    b. $y = \csc(x)$
    c. $y = \sin(x + \frac{\pi}{2})$
    d. $y = \sin(x - \frac{\pi}{2})$

29. What is the solution for the equation $\tan(x) + 1 = 0$, where $0 \leq x < 2\pi$?
    a. $x = \frac{3\pi}{4}, \frac{5\pi}{4}$
    b. $x = \frac{3\pi}{4}, \frac{\pi}{4}$
    c. $x = \frac{5\pi}{4}, \frac{7\pi}{4}$
    d. $x = \frac{3\pi}{4}, \frac{7\pi}{4}$

30. Which of the following inequalities is equivalent to $3 - \frac{1}{2}x \geq 2$?
    a. $x \geq 2$
    b. $x \leq 2$
    c. $x \geq 1$
    d. $x \leq 1$

31. For which of the following are $x = 4$ and $x = -4$ solutions?
    a. $x^2 + 16 = 0$
    b. $x^2 + 4x - 4 = 0$
    c. $x^2 - 2x - 2 = 0$
    d. $x^2 - 16 = 0$

32. If *x* is not zero, then $\frac{3}{x} + \frac{5u}{2x} - \frac{u}{4} =$

a. $\frac{12+10u-ux}{4x}$

b. $\frac{3+5u-ux}{x}$

c. $\frac{12x+10u+ux}{4x}$

d. $\frac{12+10u-u}{4x}$

33. Which of the following shows the correct result of simplifying the following expression?

$$(7n + 3n^3 + 3) + (8n + 5n^3 + 2n^4)$$

a. $9n^4 + 15n - 2$
b. $2n^4 + 5n^3 + 15n - 2$
c. $9n^4 + 8n^3 + 15n$
d. $2n^4 + 8n^3 + 15n + 3$

Reading Comprehension

1. Technology has been invading cars for the last several years, but there are some new high tech trends that are pretty amazing. It is now standard in many car models to have a rear-view camera, hands-free phone and text, and a touch screen digital display. Music can be streamed from a paired cell phone, and some displays can even be programmed with a personal photo. Sensors beep to indicate there is something in the driver's path when reversing and changing lanes. Rain-sensing windshield wipers and lights are automatic, leaving the driver with little to do but watch the road and enjoy the ride. The next wave of technology will include cars that automatically parallel park, and a self-driving car is on the horizon. These technological advances make it a good time to be a driver.

It can be concluded from this paragraph that:

a. Technology will continue to influence how cars are made.
b. Windshield wipers and lights are always automatic.
c. It is standard to have a rear-view camera in all cars.
d. Technology has reached its peak in cars.

Questions 2 and 3 refer to the following paragraph:

Caribbean Island Destinations

Do you want to vacation at a Caribbean island destination? Who wouldn't want a tropical vacation? Visit one of the many Caribbean islands where visitors can swim in crystal blue waters, swim with dolphins, or enjoy family-friendly or adult-only resorts and activities. Every island offers a unique and picturesque vacation destination. Choose from these islands: Aruba, St. Lucia, Barbados, Anguilla, St. John, and so many more. A Caribbean island destination will be the best and most refreshing vacation ever . . . no regrets!

2. What is the topic of the passage?

a. Caribbean island destinations
b. Tropical vacation
c. Resorts
d. Activities

3. What is/are the supporting detail(s) of this passage?

a. Cruising to the Caribbean
b. Local events
c. Family or adult-only resorts and activities
d. All of the above

Questions 4 and 5 refer to the following paragraph:

The Brookside area is an older part of Kansas City, developed mainly in the 1920s and 30s, and is considered one of the nation's first "planned" communities with shops, restaurants, parks, and churches all within a quick walk. A stroll down any street reveals charming two-story Tudor and Colonial homes with smaller bungalows sprinkled throughout the beautiful tree-lined streets. It is common to see lemonade stands on the corners and baseball games in the numerous "pocket" parks tucked neatly behind rows of well-manicured houses. The Brookside shops on 63rd street between Wornall Road and Oak Street are a hub of commerce and entertainment where residents freely shop and dine with their pets (and children) in tow. This is also a common "hangout" spot for younger teenagers because it is easily accessible by bike for most. In short, it is an idyllic neighborhood just minutes from downtown Kansas City.

4. Which of the following states the main idea of this paragraph?
   a. The Brookside shops are a popular hangout for teenagers.
   b. There are a number of pocket parks in the Brookside neighborhood.
   c. Brookside is a great place to live.
   d. Brookside has a high crime rate.

5. According to this paragraph, which of the following is unique to this neighborhood?
   a. It is old.
   b. It is in Kansas City.
   c. It has shopping.
   d. It is one of the nation's first planned communities.

Questions 6–11 are based upon the following passage:

> Fellow-citizens, pardon me, allow me to ask, why am I called upon to speak here to-day? What have I, or those I represent, to do with your national independence? Are the great principles of political freedom and of natural justice, embodied in that Declaration of Independence, extended to us? and am I, therefore, called upon to bring our humble offering to the national altar, and to confess the benefits and express devout gratitude for the blessings resulting from your independence to us?
>
> Would to God, both for your sakes and ours, ours that an affirmative answer could be truthfully returned to these questions! Then would my task be light, and my burden easy and delightful. For who is there so cold, that a nation's sympathy could not warm him? Who so obdurate and dead to the claims of gratitude, that would not thankfully acknowledge such priceless benefits? Who so stolid and selfish, that would not give his voice to swell the hallelujahs of a nation's jubilee, when the chains of servitude had been torn from his limbs? I am not that man. In a case like that, the dumb might eloquently speak, and the "lame man leap as an hart."
>
> But, such is not the state of the case. I say it with a sad sense of the disparity between us. I am not included within the pale of this glorious anniversary. Your high independence only reveals the immeasurable distance between us. The blessings in which you, this day, rejoice, are not enjoyed in common. – The rich inheritance of justice, liberty, prosperity and independence, bequeathed by your fathers, is shared by you, not by me. The sunlight that brought life and healing to you, as brought stripes and death to me. This Fourth [of] July is yours, not mine. You may rejoice, I must mourn. To drag a man in fetters into the grand illuminated temple of liberty, and call upon him to join you in joyous anthems, were inhuman mockery and sacrilegious irony. Do you mean, citizens, to mock me, by asking me to speak to-day? If so, there is a parallel to your conduct. And let me warn you that it is dangerous to copy the example of a nation whose crimes, lowering up to heaven, were thrown down by the breath of the Almighty, burying that nation in irrecoverable ruin! I can to-day take up the plaintive lament of a peeled and woe-smitten people!

By the rivers of Babylon, there we sat down.. Yea! we wept when we remembered Zion. We hanged our harps upon the willows in the midst thereof. For there, they that carried us away captive, required of us a song; and they who wasted us required of us mirth, saying, Sing us one of the songs of Zion. How can we sing the Lord's song in a strange land? If I forget thee, O Jerusalem, let my right hand forget her cunning. If I do not remember thee, let my tongue cleave to the roof of my mouth."

Excerpt from "What to the Slave is the Fourth of July?" by Frederick Douglass, 1852

6. What is the tone of the first paragraph of this passage?
   a. Incredulous
   b. Inclusive
   c. Contemplative
   d. Nonchalant

7. Which word CANNOT be used synonymously with the term *obdurate* as it is conveyed in the text below?

   Who so obdurate and dead to the claims of gratitude, that would not thankfully acknowledge such priceless benefits?

   a. Steadfast
   b. Stubborn
   c. Contented
   d. Unwavering

8. What is the central purpose of this text?
   a. To demonstrate the author's extensive knowledge of the Bible
   b. To address the hypocrisy of the Fourth of July holiday
   c. To convince wealthy landowners to adopt new holiday rituals
   d. To explain why minorities often relished the notion of segregation in government institutions

9. What statement shows the central purpose of this text?
   a. By the rivers of Babylon . . . down.
   b. Fellow citizens . . . today.
   c. I can . . . woe-smitten people.
   d. The rich inheritance of justice . . . *not by me*.

10. The statement below features an example of which of the following literary devices?

   Oh pity! Your high independence only reveals the immeasurable distance between us.

   a. Assonance
   b. Parallelism
   c. Amplification
   d. Hyperbole

11. The speaker's use of biblical references, such as "rivers of Babylon" and the "songs of Zion," helps the reader to do all of the following EXCEPT which of the following?

a. Identify with the speaker through the use of common text
b. Draw a connection between another group of people who have been affected by slavery and American slaves
c. Recognize the equivocation of the speaker and those that he represents
d. Appeal to the listener's sense of humanity

12. Which organizational style is used in the following passage?

> There are several reasons why the new student café has not been as successful as expected. One factor is that prices are higher than originally advertised, so many students cannot afford to buy food and beverages there. Also, the café closes rather early; as a result, students go out into town to other late-night gathering places rather than meeting friends at the café on campus.

a. Cause and effect order
b. Compare and contrast order
c. Spatial order
d. Time order

13. What can the reader infer from the following text from *Gulliver's Travels*?

> I would sometimes lie down, and let five or six of them dance on my hand; and at last the boys and girls would venture to come and play at hide-and-seek in my hair.

a. The children tortured Gulliver.
b. Gulliver traveled because he wanted to meet new people.
c. Gulliver is considerably larger than the children who are playing around him.
d. Gulliver has a genuine love and enthusiasm for people of all sizes.

14. David Foster Wallace's *Infinite Jest* is the holy grail of modern literature. It will stand the test of time in its relevance. Every single person who starts reading *Infinite Jest* cannot physically put down the book until completing it.

Which of the following is the main point of the passage?

a. David Foster Wallace's *Infinite Jest* is the holy grail of modern literature.
b. *Infinite Jest* is a page-turner.
c. David Foster Wallace wrote *Infinite Jest*.
d. *Infinite Jest* is a modern classic for good reason, and everybody should read it.

15. The assassination of Archduke Franz Ferdinand of Austria is often ascribed as the cause of World War I. However, the assassination merely lit the fuse in a combustible situation since many of the world powers were in complicated and convoluted military alliances. For example, England, France, and Russia entered into a mutual defense treaty seven years prior to World War I. Even without Franz Ferdinand's assassination, ______________________.

Which of the following most logically completes the passage?

a. A war between the world powers was extremely likely.
b. World War I never would have happened.
c. England, France, and Russia would have started the war.
d. Austria would have started the war.

Questions 16–20 are based on the following passages.

Passage I

Lethal force, or deadly force, is defined as the physical means to cause death or serious harm to another individual. The law holds that lethal force is only accepted when you or another person are in immediate and unavoidable danger of death or severe bodily harm. For example, a person could be beating someone in such a way that the victim is suffering severe trauma that could result in death or serious harm. This would be an instance where lethal force would be acceptable and possibly the only way to save the victim from irrevocable damage.

Another example of when to use lethal force would be when someone enters your home with a deadly weapon. The intruder's presence and possession of the weapon indicate mal-intent and the ability to inflict death or severe injury to you and your loved ones. Again, lethal force can be used in this situation. Lethal force can also be applied to prevent the harm of another individual. If a woman is being brutally assaulted and is unable to fend off an attacker, lethal force can be used to defend her as a last-ditch effort. If she is in immediate jeopardy of rape, harm, and/or death, lethal force could be the only response that could effectively deter the assailant.

The key to understanding the concept of lethal force is the term *last resort*. Deadly force cannot be taken back; it should be used only to prevent severe harm or death. The law does distinguish whether the means of one's self-defense is fully warranted, or if the individual goes out of control in the process. If you continually attack the assailant after they are rendered incapacitated, this would be causing unnecessary harm, and the law can bring charges against you. Likewise, if you kill an attacker unnecessarily after defending yourself, you can be charged with murder. This would move lethal force beyond necessary defense, making it no longer a last resort but rather a use of excessive force.

Passage II

Assault is the unlawful attempt of one person to apply apprehension on another individual by an imminent threat or by initiating offensive contact. Assaults can vary, encompassing physical strikes, threatening body language, and even provocative language. In the case of the latter, even if a hand has not been laid, it is still considered an assault because of its threatening nature.

Let's look at an example: A homeowner is angered because his neighbor blows fallen leaves into his freshly mowed lawn. Irate, the homeowner gestures a fist to his neighbor and threatens to bash his head in for littering on his lawn. The homeowner's physical motions and verbal threats herald a physical threat against the other neighbor. These factors classify the homeowner's reaction as an assault. If the angry neighbor hits the threatening homeowner in retaliation, that would constitute an assault as well because he physically hit the homeowner.

Assault also centers on the involvement of weapons in a conflict. If someone fires a gun at another person, it could be interpreted as an assault unless the shooter acted in self-defense. If an individual drew a gun or a knife on someone with the intent to harm them, it would be considered assault. However, it's also considered an assault if someone simply aimed a weapon, loaded or not, at another person in a threatening manner.

16. What is the purpose of the second passage?
    a. To inform the reader about what assault is and how it is committed
    b. To inform the reader about how assault is a minor example of lethal force
    c. To argue that the use of assault is more common than the use of lethal force
    d. To recount an incident in which the author was assaulted

17. Which of the following situations, according to the passages, would not constitute an illegal use of lethal force?
    a. A disgruntled cashier yells obscenities at a customer.
    b. A thief is seen running away with stolen cash.
    c. A man is attacked in an alley by another man with a knife.
    d. A woman punches another woman in a bar.

18. Given the information in the passages, which of the following must be true about assault?
    a. All assault is considered an expression of lethal force.
    b. There are various forms of assault.
    c. Assault is justified only as a last resort.
    d. Assault charges are more severe than unnecessary use of force charges.

19. Which of the following, if true, would most seriously undermine the explanation proposed by the author in the third paragraph of Passage I?
    a. An instance of lethal force in self-defense is not absolutely absolved from blame. The law takes into account the necessary use of force at the time it is committed.
    b. An individual who uses lethal force only in necessary defense is in direct compliance with the law under most circumstances.
    c. Lethal force in self-defense should be forgiven in all cases for the peace of mind of the primary victim.
    d. The use of lethal force is not evaluated on the intent of the user but rather the severity of the primary attack that warranted self-defense.

20. Based on the passages, what can we infer about the relationship between assault and lethal force?
    a. An act of lethal force always leads to a type of assault.
    b. Assault and lethal force have no conceivable connection.
    c. An assault with deadly intent can lead to an individual using lethal force to preserve their well-being.
    d. If someone uses self-defense in a conflict, it is called deadly force; if actions or threats are intended, it is called assault.

Questions 21–25 are based upon the following passage:

This excerpt is adapted from *Our Vanishing Wildlife,* by William T. Hornaday

> Three years ago, I think there were not many bird-lovers in the United States who believed it possible to prevent the total extinction of both egrets from our fauna. All the known rookeries accessible to plume-hunters had been totally destroyed. Two years ago, the secret discovery of several small, hidden colonies prompted William Dutcher, President of the National Association of Audubon Societies, and Mr. T. Gilbert Pearson, Secretary, to attempt the protection of those colonies. With a fund contributed for the

purpose, wardens were hired and duly commissioned. As previously stated, one of those wardens was shot dead in cold blood by a plume hunter. The task of guarding swamp rookeries from the attacks of money-hungry desperadoes to whom the accursed plumes were worth their weight in gold, is a very chancy proceeding. There is now one warden in Florida who says that "before they get my rookery they will first have to get me."

Thus far the protective work of the Audubon Association has been successful. Now there are twenty colonies, which contain all told, about 5,000 egrets and about 120,000 herons and ibises which are guarded by the Audubon wardens. One of the most important is on Bird Island, a mile out in Orange Lake, central Florida, and it is ably defended by Oscar E. Baynard. To-day, the plume hunters who do not dare to raid the guarded rookeries are trying to study out the lines of flight of the birds, to and from their feeding-grounds, and shoot them in transit. Their motto is—"Anything to beat the law, and get the plumes." It is there that the state of Florida should take part in the war.

The success of this campaign is attested by the fact that last year a number of egrets were seen in eastern Massachusetts—for the first time in many years. And so to-day the question is, can the wardens continue to hold the plume-hunters at bay?

Our Vanishing Wildlife, by William T. Hornaday

21. The author's use of first-person pronouns in the following text does NOT have which of the following effects?

Three years ago, I think there were not many bird-lovers in the United States who believed it possible to prevent the total extinction of both egrets from our fauna.

a. The phrase *I think* acts as a sort of hedging, where the author's tone is less direct and/or absolute.
b. It allows the reader to more easily connect with the author.
c. It encourages the reader to empathize with the egrets.
d. It distances the reader from the text by overemphasizing the story.

22. What purpose does the quote serve at the end of the first paragraph?

a. The quote shows proof of a hunter threatening one of the wardens.
b. The quote lightens the mood by illustrating the colloquial language of the region.
c. The quote provides an example of a warden protecting one of the colonies.
d. The quote provides much needed comic relief in the form of a joke.

23. What is the meaning of the word *rookeries* in the following text?

To-day, the plume hunters who do not dare to raid the guarded rookeries are trying to study out the lines of flight of the birds, to and from their feeding-grounds, and shoot them in transit.

a. Houses in a slum area
b. A place where hunters gather to trade tools
c. A place where wardens go to trade stories
d. A colony of breeding birds

24. What is on Bird Island?
    a. Hunters selling plumes
    b. An important bird colony
    c. Bird Island Battle between the hunters and the wardens
    d. An important egret with unique plumes

25. What is the main purpose of the passage?
    a. To persuade the audience to act in preservation of the bird colonies
    b. To show the effect hunting egrets has had on the environment
    c. To argue that the preservation of bird colonies has had a negative impact on the environment
    d. To demonstrate the success of the protective work of the Audubon Association

Directions for questions 1–6: Read the statement or passage and then choose the best answer to the question. Answer the question based on what is stated or implied in the statement or passage.

26. There are two major kinds of cameras on the market right now for amateur photographers. Camera enthusiasts can either purchase a digital single-lens reflex camera (DSLR) camera or a compact system camera (CSC). The main difference between a DSLR and a CSC is that the DSLR has a full-sized sensor, which means it fits in a much larger body. The CSC uses a mirrorless system, which makes for a lighter, smaller camera. While both take quality pictures, the DSLR generally has better picture quality due to the larger sensor. CSCs still take very good quality pictures and are more convenient to carry than a DSLR. This makes the CSC an ideal choice for the amateur photographer looking to step up from a point-and-shoot camera.

What is the main difference between the DSLR and CSC?
    a. The picture quality is better in the DSLR.
    b. The CSC is less expensive than the DSLR.
    c. The DSLR is a better choice for amateur photographers.
    d. The DSLR's larger sensor makes it a bigger camera than the CSC.

27. When selecting a career path, it's important to explore the various options available. Many students entering college may shy away from a major because they don't know much about it. For example, many students won't opt for a career as an actuary, because they aren't exactly sure what it entails. They would be missing out on a career that is very lucrative and in high demand. Actuaries work in the insurance field and assess risks and premiums. The average salary of an actuary is $100,000 per year. Another career option students may avoid, due to lack of knowledge of the field, is a hospitalist. This is a physician that specializes in the care of patients in a hospital, as opposed to those seen in private practices. The average salary of a hospitalist is upwards of $200,000. It pays to do some digging and find out more about these lesser-known career fields.

What is an actuary?
    a. A doctor who works in a hospital
    b. The same as a hospitalist
    c. An insurance agent who works in a hospital
    d. A person who assesses insurance risks and premiums

28. Hard water occurs when rainwater mixes with minerals from rock and soil. Hard water has a high mineral count, including calcium and magnesium. The mineral deposits from hard water can stain hard surfaces in bathrooms and kitchens as well as clog pipes. Hard water can stain dishes, ruin clothes, and reduce the life of any appliances it touches, such as hot water heaters, washing machines, and humidifiers.

One solution is to install a water softener to reduce the mineral content of water, but this can be costly. Running vinegar through pipes and appliances and using vinegar to clean hard surfaces can also help with mineral deposits.

From this passage, what can be concluded?

a. Hard water can cause a lot of problems for homeowners.
b. Calcium is good for pipes and hard surfaces.
c. Water softeners are easy to install.
d. Vinegar is the only solution to hard water problems.

29. Coaches of kids' sports teams are increasingly concerned about the behavior of parents at games. Parents are screaming and cursing at coaches, officials, players, and other parents. Physical fights have even broken out at games. Parents need to be reminded that coaches are volunteers, giving up their time and energy to help kids develop in their chosen sport. The goal of kids' sports teams is to learn and develop skills, but it's also to have fun. When parents are out of control at games and practices, it takes the fun out of the sport.

From this passage, what can be concluded?

a. Coaches are modeling good behavior for kids.
b. Organized sports are not good for kids.
c. Parents' behavior at their kids' games needs to change.
d. Parents and coaches need to work together.

30. While scientists aren't entirely certain why tornadoes form, they have some clues into the process. Tornadoes are dangerous funnel clouds that occur during a large thunderstorm. When warm, humid air near the ground meets cold, dry air from above, a column of the warm air can be drawn up into the clouds. Winds at different altitudes blowing at different speeds make the column of air rotate. As the spinning column of air picks up speed, a funnel cloud is formed. This funnel cloud moves rapidly and haphazardly. Rain and hail inside the cloud cause it to touch down, creating a tornado. Tornadoes move in a rapid and unpredictable pattern, making them extremely destructive and dangerous. Scientists continue to study tornadoes to improve radar detection and warning times.

The main purpose of this passage is to do which of the following?

a. Show why tornadoes are dangerous.
b. Explain how a tornado forms.
c. Compare thunderstorms to tornadoes.
d. Explain what to do in the event of a tornado.

31. Vacationers looking for a perfect experience should opt out of Disney parks and try a trip on Disney Cruise Lines. While a park offers rides, characters, and show experiences, it also includes long lines, often very hot weather, and enormous crowds. A Disney Cruise, on the other hand, is a relaxing, luxurious vacation that includes many of the same experiences as the parks, minus the crowds and lines. The cruise has top-notch food, maid service, water slides, multiple pools, Broadway-quality shows, and

daily character experiences for kids. There are also many activities, such as bingo, trivia contests, and dance parties that can entertain guests of all ages. The cruise even stops at Disney's private island for a beach barbecue with characters, waterslides, and water sports. Those looking for the Disney experience without the hassle should book a Disney cruise.

The main purpose of this passage is to do which of the following?

a. Explain how to book a Disney cruise.
b. Show what Disney parks have to offer.
c. Show why Disney parks are expensive.
d. Compare Disney parks to a Disney cruise.

Questions 32-34 are based on the following passage:

Christopher Columbus is often credited for discovering America. This is incorrect. First, it is impossible to "discover" something where people already live; however, Christopher Columbus did explore places in the New World that were previously untouched by Europe, so the term "explorer" would be more accurate. Another correction must be made, as well: Christopher Columbus was not the first European explorer to reach the present-day Americas! Rather, it was Leif Erikson who first came to the New World and contacted the natives, nearly five hundred years before Christopher Columbus.

Leif Erikson, the son of Erik the Red (a famous Viking outlaw and explorer in his own right), was born in either 970 or 980, depending on which historian you read. His own family, though, did not raise Leif, which was a Viking tradition. Instead, one of Erik's prisoners taught Leif reading and writing, languages, sailing, and weaponry. At age 12, Leif was considered a man and returned to his family. He killed a man during a dispute shortly after his return, and the council banished the Erikson clan to Greenland.

In 999, Leif left Greenland and traveled to Norway where he would serve as a guard to King Olaf Tryggvason. It was there that he became a convert to Christianity. Leif later tried to return home with the intention of taking supplies and spreading Christianity to Greenland, however his ship was blown off course and he arrived in a strange new land: present day Newfoundland, Canada.

When he finally returned to his adopted homeland Greenland, Leif consulted with a merchant who had also seen the shores of this previously unknown land we now know as Canada. The son of the legendary Viking explorer then gathered a crew of 35 men and set sail. Leif became the first European to touch foot in the New World as he explored present-day Baffin Island and Labrador, Canada. His crew called the land Vinland since it was plentiful with grapes.

During their time in present-day Newfoundland, Leif's expedition made contact with the natives whom they referred to as Skraelings (which translates to "wretched ones" in Norse). There are several secondhand accounts of their meetings. Some contemporaries described trade between the peoples. Other accounts describe clashes where the Skraelings defeated the Viking explorers with long spears, while still others claim the Vikings dominated the natives. Regardless of the circumstances, it seems that the Vikings made contact of some kind. This happened around 1,000, nearly five hundred years before Columbus famously sailed the ocean blue.

Eventually, in 1003, Leif set sail for home and arrived at Greenland with a ship full of timber. In 1020, seventeen years later, the legendary Viking died. Many believe that Leif Erikson should receive more credit for his contributions in exploring the New World.

32. Which of the following is an opinion, rather than historical fact, expressed by the author?
    a. Leif Erikson was definitely the son of Erik the Red; however, historians debate the year of his birth.
    b. Leif Erikson's crew called the land Vinland since it was plentiful with grapes.
    c. Leif Erikson deserves more credit for his contributions in exploring the New World.
    d. Leif Erikson explored the Americas nearly five hundred years before Christopher Columbus.

33. Which of the following most accurately describes the author's main conclusion?
    a. Leif Erikson is a legendary Viking explorer.
    b. Leif Erikson deserves more credit for exploring America hundreds of years before Columbus.
    c. Spreading Christianity motivated Leif Erikson's expeditions more than any other factor.
    d. Leif Erikson contacted the natives nearly five hundred years before Columbus.

34. Which of the following can be logically inferred from the passage?
    a. The Vikings disliked exploring the New World.
    b. Leif Erikson's banishment from Iceland led to his exploration of present-day Canada.
    c. Leif Erikson never shared his stories of exploration with the King of Norway.
    d. Historians have difficulty definitively pinpointing events in the Vikings' history

Questions 35 and 36 are based upon the following passage:

The Global Water Crisis

For decades, the world's water supply has been decreasing. At least ten percent of the world population, or over 780 million people, do not have access to potable water. They have to walk for miles, carrying heavy buckets in intense heat in order to obtain the essential life source that comes freely from our faucets.

We are in a global water crisis. Only 2.5% of the water on Earth is suitable for drinking, and over seventy percent of this water is frozen in the polar ice caps, while much of the rest is located deep underground. This leaves a very small percentage available for drinking, yet we see millions of gallons of water wasted on watering huge lawns in deserts like Arizona, or on running dishwashers that are only half-full, or on filling all the personal pools in Los Angeles, meanwhile people in Africa are dying of thirst.

In order to reduce water waste, Americans and citizens of other first world countries should adhere to the following guidelines: run the dishwasher only when it is full, do only full loads of laundry, wash the car with a bucket and not with a hose, take showers only when necessary, swim in public pools, and just be <u>cognizant</u> of how much water they are using in general. Our planet is getting thirstier by the year, and if we do not solve this problem, our species will surely perish.

35. Which of the following best supports the assertion that we need to limit our water usage?
    a. People are wasting water on superfluous things.
    b. There is very little water on Earth suitable for drinking.
    c. At least ten percent of the world population does not have access to drinking water.
    d. There is plenty of drinking water in first world countries, but not anywhere else.

36. Which of the following, if true, would challenge the assertion that we are in a global water crisis?
    a. There are abundant water stores on Earth that scientists are not reporting.
    b. Much of the water we drink comes from rain.
    c. People in Africa only have to walk less than a mile to get water.
    d. Most Americans only run the dishwasher when it is full.

Answer Explanations #1

Algebra and Functions

1. B: The equation can be solved by factoring the numerator into $(x+6)(x-5)$. Since that same factor $(x-5)$ exists on top and bottom, that factor cancels. This leaves the equation $x+6=11$. Solving the equation gives the answer $x=5$. When this value is plugged into the equation, it yields a zero in the denominator of the fraction. Since this is undefined, there is no solution.

2. D: The slope is given by the change in y divided by the change in x. Specifically, it's:

$$\text{slope} = \frac{y_2 - y_1}{x_2 - x_1}$$

The first point is $(-5, -3)$, and the second point is $(0, -1)$. Work from left to right when identifying coordinates. Thus the point on the left is point 1 $(-5, -3)$ and the point on the right is point 2 $(0, -1)$.

Now we need to just plug those numbers into the equation:

$$slope = \frac{-1-(-3)}{0-(-5)}$$

It can be simplified to:

$$slope = \frac{-1+3}{0+5}$$

$$slope = \frac{2}{5}$$

3. A: The first step is to determine the unknown, which is in terms of the length, l.

The second step is to translate the problem into the equation using the perimeter of a rectangle, $P = 2l + 2w$. The width is the length minus 2 centimeters. The resulting equation is $2l + 2(l-2) = 44$. The equation can be solved as follows:

$2l + 2l - 4 = 44$	Apply the distributive property on the left side of the equation
$4l - 4 = 44$	Combine like terms on the left side of the equation
$4l = 48$	Add 4 to both sides of the equation
$l = 12$	Divide both sides of the equation by 4

The length of the rectangle is 12 centimeters. The width is the length minus 2 centimeters, which is 10 centimeters. Checking the answers for length and width forms the following equation:

$$44 = 2(12) + 2(10)$$

The equation can be solved using the order of operations to form a true statement: $44 = 44$.

4. B: To be directly proportional means that $y = kx$. If x is changed from 5 to 20, the value of x is multiplied by 4. Applying the same rule to the y-value, also multiply the value of y by 4. Therefore:

$$y = 12$$

5. D: Solve a linear inequality in a similar way to solving a linear equation. First, start by distributing the -3 on the left side of the inequality.

$$-3x - 12 \geq x + 8$$

Then, add 12 to both sides.

$$-3x \geq x + 20$$

Next, subtract x from both sides.

$$-4x \geq 20$$

Finally, divide both sides of the inequality by -4. Don't forget to flip the inequality sign because you are dividing by a negative.

$$x \leq -5$$

6. D: Denote the width as w and the length as l. Then, $l = 3w + 5$. The perimeter is $2w + 2l = 90$. Substituting the first expression for l into the second equation yields:

$$2(3w + 5) + 2w = 90$$

$$6w + 10 + 2w = 90$$

$$8w = 80$$

$$w = 10$$

Putting this into the first equation, it yields:

$$l = 3(10) + 5 = 35$$

7. C: The The formula for continually compounded interest is:

$$A = Pe^{rt}$$

Plugging in the given values to find the total amount in the account yields the equation:

$$A = 2000e^{0.05\times 8} = 2983.65$$

Choice *A* is incorrect because it uses annually compounded interest instead of continuous,

$$A = 2000 \times 1.05^8 = 2954.91$$

Choice *B* is incorrect because it fails to apply the formula for continuously compounded interest. Choice *D* is incorrect because it simply adds 40% (or eight times 5%) to the original investment rather than compounding annually.

8. A: Let the unknown score be x. The average will be:

$$\frac{5 \times 50 + 4 \times 70 + x}{10} = \frac{530 + x}{10} = 55$$

Multiply both sides by 10 to get $530 + x = 550$, or $x = 20$.

9. A: The cumulative exponential distribution with $\lambda = 50$ should be used. One minute represents 0.017 hour. Therefore, P(arrival time less than 1 minute) = $1 - e^{-(50)(0.017)} = 0.573 = 57.3\%$. The closest answer is 57%.

10. A: To solve for x the steps are as follows:

$$4x - 12 = -2x$$

$$6x - 12 = 0$$

$$6x = 12$$

$$x = 2$$

11. D: Dividing rational expressions follows the same rule as dividing fractions. The division is changed to multiplication by the reciprocal of the second fraction. This turns the expression into:

$$\frac{5x^3}{3x^2y} \times \frac{3y^9}{25}$$

This can be simplified by finding common factors in the numerators and denominators of the two fractions.

$$\frac{x^3}{x^2y} \times \frac{y^9}{5}$$

Multiplying across creates:

$$\frac{x^3y^9}{5x^2y}$$

Simplifying leads to the final expression is:

$$\frac{xy^8}{5}$$

12. C: 216 cm^2. Because area is a two-dimensional measurement, the dimensions are multiplied by a scale factor that is squared to determine the scale factor of the corresponding areas. The dimensions of the rectangle are multiplied by a scale factor of 3. Therefore, the area is multiplied by a scale factor of 3^2 (which is equal to 9):

$$24 \text{ cm}^2 \times 9 = 216 \text{ cm}^2$$

13. D: When an ordered pair is reflected over an axis, the sign of one of the coordinates must change. When it's reflected over the x-axis, the sign of the y-coordinate must change. The x-value remains the same. Therefore, the new ordered pair is $(-3, 4)$.

14. D: 3 times the sum of a number and 7 is greater than or equal to 32 can be translated into equation form utilizing mathematical operators and numbers.

15. C: To find the mean, or average, of a set of values, add the values together and then divide by the total number of values. Each day of the week has an adult ticket amount sold that must be added together. The equation is as follows:

$$\frac{22 + 16 + 24 + 19 + 29}{5} = 22$$

16. D: First, convert the distance that Courtney already drove to feet. Because there are three feet per yard, her distance traveled thus far in yards must be multiplied by 3:

$$1{,}236 \times 3 = 3{,}708 \text{ feet}$$

If the total distance to travel is 6,292 feet, there is $6292 - 3708 = 2{,}584$ feet left to travel.

17. B: The number line shows $x > -\frac{3}{4}$. Each inequality must be solved for x to determine if it matches the number line.

Choice *A* of $4x + 5 < 8$ results in $x < -\frac{3}{4}$, which is incorrect.

Choice *C* of $-4x + 5 > 8$ yields $x < -\frac{3}{4}$, which is also incorrect.

Choice *D* of $4x - 5 > 8$ results in $x > \frac{13}{4}$, which is not correct.

Choice B, $-4x + 5 < 8$ is the only choice that results in the correct answer of $x > -\frac{3}{4}$

18. C: The equation used to find the slope of a line when given two points is as follows:

$$slope = \frac{y_2 - y_1}{x_2 - x_1}$$

Substituting the points into the equation yields:

$$\frac{8 - (-4)}{-5 - 10}$$

$$\frac{12}{-15}$$

$$-\frac{4}{5}$$

19. D: The length of LM can be found by a series of calculations:

$$KL + LM = 16 \qquad KL = 16 - LM$$

$$LM + MN = 20 \qquad MN = 20 - LM$$

$$KN = KL + MN + LM = 30$$

$$16 - LM + 20 - LM + LM = 30$$

$$36 - 30 = LM$$

$$6 = LM$$

20. C: Each value can be calculated so that they can be compared to find which one is the greatest. The mean is equal to:

$$\frac{26 + 27 + 27 + 29 + 30 + 32 + 33 + 33 + 33 + 35}{10} = 30.5$$

The median is equal to:

$$\frac{30 + 32}{2} = 31$$

The mode is equal to 33 because that number occurs 3 times in the data set. The range is equal to:

$$35 - 26 = 9$$

Therefore, the mode is the greatest value of the answer choices.

21. B: When the number of data points provided is an even number, then the average of the two middle points is the median. Each set of responses provided should be ordered from least to greatest, and then the middle two values should be averaged together to see which set provides a median of 14. Choice *B,* when ordered, is 11, 12, 13, 15, 16, and 16. The middle two values averaged together is:

$$\frac{13 + 15}{2} = 14 \text{ miles}$$

This is the correct answer.

22. B: Start with the original equation: $x^2 - 2xy + 2y$, then replace each instance of x with a 2, and each instance of y with a 3 to get:

$$2^2 - 2 \times 2 \times 3 + 2 \times 3^2 = 4 - 12 + 18 = 10$$

23. A: To expand a squared binomial, it's necessary to use the First, Outer, Inner, Last (FOIL) Method.

$$(2x - 4y)^2$$

$$(2x)(2x) + (2x)(-4y) + (-4y)(2x) + (-4y)(-4y)$$

$$4x^2 - 8xy - 8xy + 16y^2$$

$$4x^2 - 16xy + 16y^2$$

24. D: Factor the numerator into $x^2 - 6x + 9 = (x-3)^2$, since:

$$-3 - 3 = -6$$

$$(-3)(-3) = 9$$

Factor the denominator into $x^2 - x - 6 = (x-3)(x+2)$, since:

$$-3 + 2 = -1,$$

$$(-3)(2) = -6$$

This means the rational function can be rewritten as:

$$\frac{x^2 - 6x + 9}{x^2 - x - 6} = \frac{(x-3)^2}{(x-3)(x+2)}$$

Using the restriction of x > 3, do not worry about any of these terms being 0, and cancel an $x - 3$ from the numerator and the denominator, leaving $\frac{x-3}{x+2}$.

25. B: Add 3 to both sides to get $4x = 8$. Then divide both sides by 4 to get $x = 2$.

26. B: There are two zeros for the given function. They are $x = 0, -2$. The zeros can be found several ways, but this particular equation can be factored into:

$$f(x) = x(x^2 + 4x + 4) = x(x+2)(x+2)$$

By setting each factor equal to zero and solving for x, there are two solutions: $x = 0$ and $x = -2$. On a graph, these zeros can be seen where the line crosses the x-axis.

27. D: This problem involves a composition function, where one function is plugged into the other function. In this case, the $f(x)$ function is plugged into the $g(x)$ function for each x-value. The composition equation becomes:

$$g(f(x)) = 2^3 - 3(2^2) - 2(2) + 6$$

Simplifying the equation gives the answer:

$$g(f(x)) = 8 - 3(4) - 2(2) + 6 = 8 - 12 - 4 + 6 = -2$$

28. C: Graphing the function $y = \cos(x)$ shows that the curve starts at $(0, 1)$, has an amplitude of 2, and a period of 2π. This same curve can be constructed using the sine graph, by shifting the graph to the left $\frac{\pi}{2}$ units. This equation is in the form:

$$y = \sin(x + \frac{\pi}{2})$$

29. D: Using SOHCAHTOA, tangent is $\frac{y}{x}$ for the special triangles. Since the value of $\tan(x)$ needs to be negative one, the angle for the tangent must be some form of 45 degrees or $\frac{\pi}{4}$. The value is negative in the second and fourth quadrant, so the answer is $\frac{3\pi}{4}$ and $\frac{7\pi}{4}$.

30. B: To simplify this inequality, subtract 3 from both sides to get:

$$-\frac{1}{2}x \geq -1$$

Then, multiply both sides by -2 (remembering that this flips the direction of the inequality) to get $x \leq 2$.

31. D: There are two ways to approach this problem. Each value can be substituted into each equation. A can be eliminated, since:

$$4^2 + 16 = 32$$

Choice *B* can be eliminated, since:

$$4^2 + 4 \cdot 4 - 4 = 28$$

C can be eliminated, since

$$4^2 - 2 \cdot 4 - 2 = 6$$

But, plugging in either value into $x^2 - 16$, which gives:

$$(\pm 4)^2 - 16 = 16 - 16 = 0$$

32. A: The common denominator here will be $4x$. Rewrite these fractions as:

$$\frac{3}{x} + \frac{5u}{2x} - \frac{u}{4}$$

$$\frac{12}{4x} + \frac{10u}{4x} - \frac{ux}{4x}$$

$$\frac{12x + 10u - ux}{4x}$$

33. D: The expression is simplified by collecting like terms. Terms with the same variable and exponent are like terms, and their coefficients can be added.

Reading Comprehension

1. A: The passage discusses recent technological advances in cars and suggests that this trend will continue in the future with self-driving cars. Choice *B* and *C* are not true, so these are both incorrect. Choice *D* is also incorrect because the passage suggests continuing growth in technology, not a peak.

2. A: The topic of the passage is Caribbean island destinations. The *topic* of the passage can be described in a one- or two-word phrase. Remember, when paraphrasing a passage, it is important to include the topic. Paraphrasing is when one puts a passage into their own words.

3. C: Family or adult-only resorts and activities are supporting details in this passage. *Supporting details* are details that help readers better understand the main idea. They answer questions such as who, what, where, when, why, or how. In this question, cruises and local events are not discussed in the passage, whereas family and adult-only resorts and activities support the main idea.

4. C: All the details in this paragraph suggest that Brookside is a great place to live, plus the last sentence states that it is an *idyllic neighborhood*, meaning it is perfect, happy, and blissful. Choices *A* and *B* are incorrect, because although they do contain specific details from the paragraph that support the main idea, they are not the main idea. Choice *D* is incorrect because there is no reference in the paragraph to the crime rate in Brookside.

5. D: In the first sentence, it states very clearly that the Brookside neighborhood is *one of the nation's first planned communities*. This makes it unique, as many other neighborhoods are old, many other neighborhoods exist in Kansas City, and many other neighborhoods have shopping areas. For these reasons, all the other answer choices are incorrect.

6. A: The tone is incredulous. While contemplative is an option because of the inquisitive nature of the text, Choice A is correct because Frederick Douglass is astonished that he, a former slave, would be called upon to celebrate liberty that was not extended to him or to others of his race. Choice B is incorrect because Frederick Douglass is drawing contrasts between two groups of people rather than being inclusive. Choice C is incorrect because Frederick Douglass is expressing strong emotion, incredulity, rather than contemplation. Choice D is incorrect because Frederick Douglass is not nonchalant, nor accepting of the circumstances which he describes.

7. C: Choice C, contented, is the only word that has the opposite meaning of obdurate. Therefore, Choices A, B, and D are incorrect.

8. B: While the speaker makes biblical references, it is not the main focus of the passage, thus eliminating Choice *A* as an answer. The passage also makes no mention of wealthy landowners and doesn't speak of any positive response to the historical events, so Choices *C* and *D* are not correct.

9. D: Choice D is the correct answer because it clearly references the disparity between slaves and free men in the United States. Choice A is incorrect because it demonstrates Frederick Douglass's knowledge of the Bible. Choice B is incorrect because it demonstrates his incredulity at his invitation to speak. Choice C is incorrect because Frederick Douglass is highlighting the terrible situation of slaves, but he is not highlighting the disparity between slaves and free men.

10. D: It is an example of hyperbole; the physical distance between Frederick Douglass and his audience was not, in fact, immeasurable. However, it clearly demonstrated the differences in the lives and situations of free men and slaves in the United States. Choice A is incorrect because assonance is the repetition of sounds and commonly occurs in poetry. Choice B is incorrect because parallelism refers to two statements that correlate, or parallel each other, in some manner.

11. C: Recognize the equivocation of the speaker and those that he represents. Choice C is correct because the speaker is clear about his intention and stance throughout the text; he does not equivocate, so this answer choice is the only one that biblical references do not help the reader to do. Choice A is incorrect because quotations from the Bible would have been common at the time, creating a common ground between Frederick Douglass and his audience. Choice B is incorrect because another group of people affected by slavery are being referenced, and Frederick Douglass is clearly drawing a connection between that group of people and American slaves. Choice D is incorrect because Frederick Douglass's speech is designed to appeal to the listener's sense of humanity and create an abhorrence for slavery.

12. A: The passage describes a situation and then explains the causes that led to it. Also, it utilizes cause and effect signal words, such as *reasons, factors, so,* and *as a result*. *B* is incorrect because a compare and contrast order considers the similarities and differences of two or more things. *C* is incorrect because spatial order describes where things are located in relation to each other. Finally, *D* is incorrect because time order describes when things occurred chronologically.

13. C: Choice A is incorrect because there is no indication of stress in Gulliver's tone. Choices B and D aren't the best answer because though Gulliver seems fond of his new acquaintances, he didn't travel there with the intentions of meeting new people, nor does he express a definite love for them in this particular portion of the text.

14. D: Choice *D* looks like a strong answer. This answer choice references the argument's main points—*Infinite Jest* is a modern classic, the book deserves its praise, and everybody should read it. In contrast, Choice *A* restates the author's conclusion. The correct answer to main point questions will often be closely related to the conclusion. Choice *B* restates a premise. Is the author's main point that *Infinite Jest* is a page-turner? No, he uses readers' obsession with the book as a premise. Eliminate this choice. Choice *C* is definitely not the main point of the passage. It's a simple fact underlying the argument. It certainly cannot be considered the main point. Eliminate this choice.

15. A: Choice *A* is consistent with the argument's logic. The argument asserts that the world powers' military alliances amounted to a delicate fuse, and the assassination merely lit it. The main point of the argument is that any event involving the military alliances would have led to a world war. Choice *B* runs counter to the argument's tone and reasoning. It can immediately be eliminated. Choice *C* is also clearly incorrect. At no point does the argument blame any single or group of countries for starting World War I. Choice *D* is incorrect for the same reason as Choice *C*. Eliminate this choice.

16. A: The purpose is to inform the reader about what assault is and how it is committed. Choice *B* is incorrect because the passage does not state that assault is a lesser form of lethal force, only that an assault can use lethal force, or alternatively, lethal force can be utilized to counter a dangerous assault. Choice *C* is incorrect because the passage is informative and does not have a set agenda. Finally, Choice *D* is incorrect because although the author uses an example in order to explain assault, it is not indicated that this is the author's personal account.

17. C: The situation of the man who is attacked in an alley by another man with a knife would most merit the use of lethal force. If the man being attacked used lethal force in self-defense, it would not be considered illegal. The presence of a deadly weapon indicates mal-intent and because the individual is isolated in an alley, lethal force in self-defense may be the only way to preserve his life. Choices *A* and *B* can be ruled out because in these situations, no one is in danger of immediate death or bodily harm by someone else. Choice *D* is an assault that does exhibit intent to harm, but this situation isn't severe enough to merit lethal force; there is no intent to kill.

18. B: As discussed in the second passage, there are several forms of assault, like assault with a deadly weapon, verbal assault, or threatening posture or language. Choice *A* is incorrect because lethal force and assault are separate as indicated by the passages. Choice *C* is incorrect because assault is never justified. Self-defense resulting in lethal force can be justified. Choice *D* is incorrect because the author does mention what the charges are on assaults; therefore, we cannot assume that they are more or less than unnecessary use of force charges.

19. D: If true, the statement in Choice D would most undermine the last part of the passage because it directly contradicts how the law evaluates the use of lethal force.Choices *A* and *B* are stated in the paragraph, and therefore do not undermine the explanation from the author. Choice *C* does not necessarily undermine the passage, but it does not support the passage either. It is more of an opinion that does not strengthen or weaken the explanation.

20. C: An assault with deadly intent can lead to an individual using lethal force to preserve their well-being. Choice *C* is correct because it clearly establishes what both assault and lethal force are and gives the specific way in which the two concepts meet. Choice *A* is incorrect because lethal force doesn't necessarily result in assault. Choice *B* is incorrect because it contradicts the information in the passage (that assault with deadly intent can lead to an individual using lethal force). Choice *D* is compelling but ultimately too vague; the statement touches on aspects of the two ideas but fails to present the concrete way in which the two are connected to each other.

21. D: The use of "I" could serve to have a "hedging" effect, allow the reader to connect with the author in a more personal way, and cause the reader to empathize more with the egrets. However, it doesn't distance the reader from the text, making Choice *D* the answer to this question.

22. C: The quote provides an example of a warden protecting one of the colonies. Choice *A* is incorrect because the speaker of the quote is a warden, not a hunter. Choice *B* is incorrect because the quote does not lighten the mood but shows the danger of the situation between the wardens and the hunters. Choice *D* is incorrect because there is no humor found in the quote.

23. D: A *rookery* is a colony of breeding birds. Although *rookery* could mean Choice *A*, houses in a slum area, it does not make sense in this context. Choices *B* and *C* are both incorrect, as this is not a place for hunters to trade tools or for wardens to trade stories.

24. B: An important bird colony. The previous sentence is describing "twenty colonies" of birds, so what follows should be a bird colony. Choice *A* may be true, but we have no evidence of this in the text. Choice *C* does touch on the tension between the hunters and wardens, but there is no official "Bird Island Battle" mentioned in the text. Choice *D* does not exist in the text.

25. D: To demonstrate the success of the protective work of the Audubon Association. The text mentions several different times how and why the association has been successful and gives examples to back this fact. Choice *A* is incorrect because although the article, in some instances, calls certain people to act, it is not the purpose of the entire passage. There is no way to tell if Choices *B* and *C* are correct, as they are not mentioned in the text.

26. D: The passage directly states that the larger sensor is the main difference between the two cameras. Choices *A* and *B* may be true, but these answers do not identify the major difference between the two cameras. Choice *C* states the opposite of what the paragraph suggests is the best option for amateur photographers, so it is incorrect.

27. D: An actuary assesses risks and sets insurance premiums. While an actuary does work in insurance, the passage does not suggest that actuaries have any affiliation with hospitalists or working in a hospital, so all other choices are incorrect.

28. A: The passage focuses mainly on the problems of hard water. Choice *B* is incorrect because calcium is not good for pipes and hard surfaces. The passage does not say anything about whether water softeners are easy to install, so Choice *C* is incorrect. Choice *D* is also incorrect because the passage does offer other solutions besides vinegar.

29. C: The main point of this paragraph is that parents need to change their poor behavior at their kids' sporting events. Choice *A* is incorrect because the coaches' behavior is not mentioned in the paragraph. Choice *B* suggests that sports are bad for kids, when the paragraph is about parents' behavior, so it is incorrect. While Choice *D* may be true, it offers a specific solution to the problem, which the paragraph does not discuss.

30. B: The main point of this passage is to show how tornadoes form. Choice *A* is off base because while the passage does mention that tornadoes are dangerous, it is not the main focus of the passage. While thunderstorms are mentioned, they are not compared to tornadoes, so Choice *C* is incorrect. Choice *D* is incorrect because the passage does not discuss what to do in the event of a tornado.

31. D: The passage compares Disney cruises with Disney parks. It does not discuss how to book a cruise, so Choice *A* is incorrect. Choice *B* is incorrect because though the passage does mention some of the park attractions, it is not the main point. The passage does not mention the cost of either option, so Choice *C* is incorrect.

32. C: Choice *A* is incorrect because it describes facts: Leif Erikson was the son of Erik the Red and historians debate Leif's date of birth. These are not opinions. Choice *B* is incorrect; that Erikson called the land Vinland is a verifiable fact as is Choice *D* because he did contact the natives almost 500 years before Columbus. Choice *C* is the correct answer because it is the author's opinion that Erikson deserves more credit. That, in fact, is his conclusion in the piece, but another person could argue that Columbus or another explorer deserves more credit for opening up the New World to exploration. Rather than being an incontrovertible fact, it is a subjective value claim.

33. B: Choice *A* is incorrect because the author aims to go beyond describing Erikson as merely a legendary Viking. Choice *C* is incorrect because the author does not focus on Erikson's motivations, let alone name the spreading of Christianity as his primary objective. Choice *D* is incorrect because it is a premise that Erikson contacted the natives 500 years before Columbus, which is simply a part of supporting the author's conclusion. Choice *B* is correct because, as stated in the previous answer, it accurately identifies the author's statement that Erikson deserves more credit than he has received for being the first European to explore the New World.

34. D: Choice *A* is incorrect because the author never addresses the Vikings' state of mind or emotions. Choice *B* is incorrect because the author does not elaborate on Erikson's exile and whether he would have become an explorer if not for his banishment. Choice *C* is incorrect because there is not enough information to support this premise. It is unclear whether Erikson informed the King of Norway of his finding. Although it is true that the King did not send a follow-up expedition, he could have simply chosen not to expend the resources after receiving Erikson's news. It is not possible to logically infer whether Erikson told him. Choice *D* is correct because there are two examples—Leif Erikson's date of birth and what happened during the encounter with the natives—of historians having trouble pinning down important details in Viking history.

35. B: Choice *B* is correct because having very little drinking water on Earth is a very good reason that one should limit their water usage so that the human population does not run out of drinking water and die out. People wasting water on superfluous things does not support the fact that we need to limit our water usage. It merely states that people are wasteful. Therefore, *A* is incorrect. Answer Choice *C* may be tempting, but it is not the correct one, as this article is not about reducing water usage in order to help those who don't have easy access to water, but about the fact that the planet is running out of drinking water. Choice *D* is incorrect because nowhere in the article does it state that only first world countries have access to drinking water.

36. A: If the assertion is that the Earth does not have enough drinking water, then having abundant water stores that are not being reported would certainly challenge this assertion. Choice *B* is incorrect because even if much of the water we drink does come from rain, that means the human population would be dependent on rain in order to survive, which would more support the assertion than challenge it. Because the primary purpose of the passage is not to help those who cannot get water, then Choice *C* is not the correct answer. Even if Choice *D* were true, it does not dismiss the other ways in which people are wasteful with water, and is also not the point.

Practice Test #2

Algebra and Functions

1. How could the following equation be factored to find the zeros?

$$y = x^3 - 3x^2 - 4x$$

a. $0 = x^2(x-4), x = 0, 4$
b. $0 = 3x(x+1)(x+4), x = 0, -1, -4$
c. $0 = x(x+1)(x+6), x = 0, -1, -6$
d. $0 = x(x+1)(x-4), x = 0, -1, 4$

2. What is the simplified quotient of $\frac{5x^3}{3x^2y} \div \frac{25}{3y^9}$?

a. $\frac{125x}{9y^{10}}$
b. $\frac{x}{5y^8}$
c. $\frac{5}{xy^8}$
d. $\frac{xy^8}{5}$

3. What type of function is modeled by the values in the following table?

x	$f(x)$
1	2
2	4
3	8
4	16
5	32

a. Linear
b. Exponential
c. Quadratic
d. Cubic

4. What is the simplified form of the expression $tan\theta \ cos\theta$?

a. $sin\theta$
b. 1
c. $csc\theta$
d. $\frac{1}{sec\theta}$

5. Which equation is not a function?
   a. $y = |x|$
   b. $y = \sqrt{x}$
   c. $x = 3$
   d. $y = 4$

6. How could the following function be rewritten to identify the zeros?

$$y = 3x^3 + 3x^2 - 18x$$

   a. $y = 3x(x + 3)(x - 2)$
   b. $y = x(x - 2)(x + 3)$
   c. $y = 3x(x - 3)(x + 2)$
   d. $y = (x + 3)(x - 2)$

7. If $x^2 - x - 3 = 0$, what is the value of $\left(x - \frac{1}{2}\right)^2$?
   a. $\frac{13}{2}$
   b. $\frac{13}{4}$
   c. 13
   d. $\frac{169}{4}$

8. A ball is thrown from the top of a high hill, so that the height of the ball as a function of time is $h(t) = -16t^2 + 4t + 6$, in feet. What is the maximum height of the ball in feet?
   a. 6
   b. 6.25
   c. 6.5
   d. 6.75

9. What is the domain for the function $y = \sqrt{x}$?
   a. All real numbers
   b. $x \geq 0$
   c. $x > 0$
   d. $y \geq 0$

10. What is the inverse of the function $f(x) = 3x - 5$?
   a. $f^{-1}(x) = \frac{x}{3} + 5$
   b. $f^{-1}(x) = \frac{5x}{3}$
   c. $f^{-1}(x) = 3x + 5$
   d. $f^{-1}(x) = \frac{x+5}{3}$

11. Is the following function even, odd, neither, or both?

$$y = \frac{1}{2}x^4 + 2x^2 - 6$$

a. Even
b. Odd
c. Neither
d. Both

12. For which of the following are $x = 4$ and $x = -4$ solutions?
a. $x^2 + 16 = 0$
b. $x^2 + 4x - 4 = 0$
c. $x^2 - 2x - 2 = 0$
d. $x^2 - 16 = 0$

13. If $f(x) = 4x + 2$, and $f^{-1}(x)$ is the inverse function for f, then what is $f^{-1}(6)$?
a. 0
b. $\frac{1}{2}$
c. 1
d. $\frac{3}{2}$

14. An equation for the line passing through the origin and the point $(2, 1)$ is
a. $y = 2x$
b. $y = \frac{1}{2}x$
c. $y = x - 2$
d. $2y = x + 1$

15. What are the y-intercept(s) for $y = x^2 + 3x - 4$?
a. $y = 1$
b. $y = -4$
c. $y = 3$
d. $y = 4$

16. If $\sqrt{1 + x} = 4$, what is *x*?
a. 10
b. 15
c. 20
d. 25

17. Suppose $\frac{x+2}{x} = 2$. What is *x*?
a. -1
b. 0
c. 2
d. 4

18. If $a \neq b$, solve for x if $\frac{1}{x} + \frac{2}{a} = \frac{2}{b}$
   a. $\frac{a-b}{ab}$
   b. $\frac{ab}{2(a-b)}$
   c. $\frac{2(a-b)}{ab}$
   d. $\frac{a-b}{2ab}$

19. Let $f(x) = 2x + 1, g(x) = \frac{x-1}{4}$. Find $g(f(x))$.
   a. $\frac{x+1}{2}$
   b. $\frac{x}{2}$
   c. $\frac{2x^2-x-1}{4}$
   d. $3x$

20. If $f(x) = (\frac{1}{2})^x$ and $a < b$, then which of the following must be true?
   a. $f(a) < f(b)$
   b. $f(a) > f(b)$
   c. $f(a) + f(b) = 0$
   d $3f(a) = f(b)$

21. A line passes through the point (1, 2) and crosses the *y*-axis at *y* = 1. Which of the following is an equation for this line?
   a. $y = 2x$
   b. $y = x + 1$
   c. $x + y = 1$
   d. $y = \frac{x}{2} - 2$

22. $x^4 - 16$ can be simplified to which of the following?
   a. $(x^2 - 4)(x^2 + 4)$
   b. $(x^2 + 4)(x^2 + 4)$
   c. $(x^2 - 4)(x^2 - 4)$
   d. $(x^2 - 2)(x^2 + 4)$

23. What is the slope of the line tangent to the graph of $y = x^3 - 4$ at the point where $x = 2$?
   a. $3x^2$
   b. 4
   c. -4
   d. 12

24. Where is the function $g(x) = \frac{\sqrt{x-2}}{x^3-8}$ continuous?
   a. $[2, \infty)$
   b. $(-\infty, \infty)$
   c. $(2, \infty)$
   d. $(-\infty, 2]$

25. Find $\frac{d}{dx} 2x^3$.
   a. $8x^2$
   b. $5x$
   c. $6x^2$
   d. $\frac{x^4}{2}$

26. If $x = 2.6$ and $y = 5.3$, what is the value of $3.2xy - 4.1y$?
   a. -7.95
   b. 33.436
   c. 44.096
   d. 22.366

27. What is the solution to the radical equation $\sqrt[3]{2x + 11} + 9 = 12$?
   a. -8
   b. 8
   c. 0
   d. 12

28. What is the solution to the following system of equations?

$$\begin{cases} x^2 + y = 4 \\ 2x + y = 1 \end{cases}$$

   a. (-1, 3)
   b. (-1, 3), (3, -5)
   c. (3, -5)
   d. (-1, 3)

29. If $f(x) = x^2 - 3x + 17$, then what is $f(x + 1)$?
   a. $x^2 - 3x + 19$
   b. $x^2 - x + 15$
   c. $x^2 + 2x + 18$
   d. $x^2 - 3x + 14$

30. What is the product of the following expression?

$$(x + 2)(x^2 + 5x - 6)$$

   a. $8x^2 + 4x - 12$
   b. $x^2 + 6x - 4$
   c. $x^3 + 7x^2 + 4x - 12$
   d. $x^3 + 5x^2 - 4x - 12$

31. What are the roots of $x^2 + x - 2$?
   a. 1 and -2
   b. -1 and 2
   c. 2 and -2
   d. 9 and 13

32. What is the *y*-intercept of $y = x^{5/3} + (x - 3)(x + 1)$?
   a. 3.5
   b. 7.6
   c. -3
   d. -15.1

33. $(4x^2y^4)^{\frac{3}{2}}$ can be simplified to which of the following?
   a. $8x^3y^6$
   b. $4x^{\frac{5}{2}}y$
   c. $4xy$
   d. $32x^{\frac{7}{2}}y^{\frac{11}{2}}$

Reading Comprehension

Questions 1-6 are based upon the following passage:

"Did you ever come across a protégé of his—one Hyde?" He asked.

"Hyde?" repeated Lanyon. "No. Never heard of him. Since my time."

That was the amount of information that the lawyer carried back with him to the great, dark bed on which he tossed to and fro until the small hours of the morning began to grow large. It was a night of little ease to his toiling mind, toiling in mere darkness and besieged by questions.

Six o'clock struck on the bells of the church that was so conveniently near to Mr. Utterson's dwelling, and still he was digging at the problem. Hitherto it had touched him on the intellectual side alone; but now his imagination also was engaged, or rather enslaved; and as he lay and tossed in the gross darkness of the night in the curtained room, Mr. Enfield's tale went by before his mind in a scroll of lighted pictures. He would be aware of the great field of lamps in a nocturnal city; then of the figure of a man walking swiftly; then of a child running from the doctor's; and then these met, and that human Juggernaut trod the child down and passed on regardless of her screams. Or else he would see a room in a rich house, where his friend lay asleep, dreaming and smiling at his dreams; and then the door of that room would be opened, the curtains of the bed plucked apart, the sleeper recalled, and, lo! There would stand by his side a figure to whom power was given, and even at that dead hour he must rise and do its bidding. The figure in these two phases haunted the lawyer all night; and if at any time he dozed over, it was but to see it glide more stealthily through sleeping houses, or move the more swiftly, and still the more smoothly, even to dizziness, through wider labyrinths of lamplighted city, and at every street corner crush a child and leave her screaming. And still the figure had no face by which he might know it; even in his dreams it had no face, or one that baffled him and melted before his eyes; and thus it was that there sprung up and grew apace in the lawyer's mind a singularly strong, almost an inordinate, curiosity to behold the features of the real Mr. Hyde. If he could but once set eyes on him, he thought the mystery would lighten and perhaps roll altogether away, as was the habit of mysterious things when well examined. He might see a reason for his friend's strange preference or bondage, and even for the startling clauses of the will. And at least it would be a face worth seeing: the face of a man who was without bowels of mercy: a face which had but to show itself to raise up, in the mind of the unimpressionable Enfield, a spirit of enduring hatred.

From that time forward, Mr. Utterson began to haunt the door in the by-street of shops. In the morning before office hours, at noon when business was plenty and time scarce, at night under the face of the full city moon, by all lights and at all hours of solitude or concourse, the lawyer was to be found on his chosen post.

"If he be Mr. Hyde," he had thought, "I should be Mr. Seek."

This excerpt is an adaptation of Robert Louis Stevenson's *The Strange Case of Dr. Jekyll and Mr. Hyde*

1. What is the purpose of the use of repetition in the following passage?

It was a night of little ease to his toiling mind, toiling in mere darkness and besieged by questions.

a. It serves as a demonstration of the mental state of Mr. Lanyon.
b. It is reminiscent of the church bells that are mentioned in the story.
c. It mimics Mr. Utterson's ambivalence.
d. It emphasizes Mr. Utterson's anguish in failing to identify Hyde's whereabouts.

2. What is the setting of the story in this passage?

a. In the city
b. On the countryside
c. In a jail
d. In a mental health facility

3. What can one infer about the meaning of the word *Juggernaut* from the author's use of it in the passage?

a. It is an apparition that appears at daybreak.
b. It scares children.
c. It is associated with space travel.
d. Mr. Utterson finds it soothing.

4. What is the definition of the word *haunt* in the following passage?

From that time forward, Mr. Utterson began to haunt the door in the by-street of shops. In the morning before office hours, at noon when business was plenty and time scarce, at night under the face of the full city moon, by all lights and at all hours of solitude or concourse, the lawyer was to be found on his chosen post.

a. To levitate
b. To constantly visit
c. To terrorize
d. To daunt

5. The phrase *labyrinths of lamplighted city* contains an example of what?

a. Hyperbole
b. Simile
c. Juxtaposition
d. Alliteration

6. What can one reasonably conclude from the final comment of this passage?

"If he be Mr. Hyde," he had thought, "I should be Mr. Seek."

a. The speaker is considering a name change.
b. The speaker is experiencing an identity crisis.
c. The speaker has mistakenly been looking for the wrong person.
d. The speaker intends to continue to look for Hyde.

Questions 7–10 are based on the following passage:

Learning how to write a ten-minute play may seem like a monumental task at first; but, if you follow a simple creative writing strategy, similar to writing a narrative story, you will be able to write a successful drama. The first step is to open your story as if it is a puzzle to be solved. This will allow the reader a moment to engage with the story and to mentally solve the story with you, the author. Immediately provide descriptive details that steer the main idea, the tone, and the mood according to the overarching theme you have in mind. For example, if the play is about something ominous, you may open Scene One with a thunderclap. Next, use dialogue to reveal the attitudes and personalities of each of the characters who have a key part in the unfolding story. Keep the characters off balance in some way to create interest and dramatic effect. Maybe what the characters say does not match what they do. Show images on stage to speed up the narrative; remember, one picture speaks a thousand words. As the play progresses, the protagonist must cross the point of no return in some way; this is the climax of the story. Then, as in a written story, you create a resolution to the life-changing event of the protagonist. Let the characters experience some kind of self-discovery that can be understood and appreciated by the patient audience. Finally, make sure all things come together in the end so that every detail in the play makes sense right before the curtain falls.

7. Based on the passage above, which of the following statements is FALSE?
   a. Writing a ten-minute play may seem like an insurmountable task.
   b. Providing descriptive details is not necessary until after the climax of the story line.
   c. Engaging the audience by jumping into the story line immediately helps them solve the story's developing ideas with you, the writer.
   d. Descriptive details give clues to the play's intended mood and tone.

8. In the passage above, the writer suggests that writing a ten-minute play is accessible for a novice playwright because of which of the following reasons?
   a. It took the author of the passage only one week to write his first play.
   b. The format follows similar strategies of writing a narrative story.
   c. There are no particular themes or points to unravel; a playwright can use a stream of consciousness style to write a play.
   d. Dialogue that reveals the characters' particularities is uncommonly simple to write.

9. Based on the passage above, which basic feature of narrative writing is NOT mentioned with respect to writing a ten-minute play?
   a. Character development
   b. Descriptive details
   c. Dialogue
   d. Style

10. Based on the passage above, which of the following is true?
   a. The class of eighth graders quickly learned that it is not that difficult to write a ten-minute play.
   b. The playwrights of the twenty-first century all use the narrative writing basic feature guide to outline their initial scripts.
   c. In order to follow a simple structure, a person can write a ten-minute play based on some narrative writing features.
   d. Women find playwriting easier than men because they are used to communicating in writing.

Question 11 is based on the following passage:

A famous children's author recently published a historical fiction novel under a pseudonym; however, it did not sell as many copies as her children's books. In her earlier years, she had majored in history and earned a graduate degree in Antebellum American History, which is the time frame of her new novel. Critics praised this newest work far more than the children's series that made her famous. In fact, her new novel was nominated for the prestigious Albert J. Beveridge Award but still isn't selling like her children's books, which fly off the shelves because of her name alone.

11. Which one of the following statements might be accurately inferred based on the above passage?
    a. The famous children's author produced an inferior book under her pseudonym.
    b. The famous children's author is the foremost expert on Antebellum America.
    c. The famous children's author did not receive the bump in publicity for her historical novel that it would have received if it were written under her given name.
    d. People generally prefer to read children's series than historical fiction.

Questions 12-17 are based on the following passage:

When researchers and engineers undertake a large-scale scientific project, they may end up making discoveries and developing technologies that have far wider uses than originally intended. This is especially true in NASA, one of the most influential and innovative scientific organizations in America. NASA spinoff technology refers to innovations originally developed for NASA space projects that are now used in a wide range of different commercial fields. Many consumers are unaware that products they are buying are based on NASA research! Spinoff technology proves that it is worthwhile to invest in science research because it could enrich people's lives in unexpected ways.

The first spinoff technology worth mentioning is baby food. In space, where astronauts have limited access to fresh food and fewer options about their daily meals, malnutrition is a serious concern. Consequently, NASA researchers were looking for ways to enhance the nutritional value of astronauts' food. Scientists found that a certain type of algae could be added to food, improving the food's neurological benefits. When experts in the commercial food industry learned of this algae's potential to boost brain health, they were quick to begin their own research. The nutritional substance from algae then developed into a product called life's DHA, which can be found in over 90% of infant food sold in America.

Another intriguing example of a spinoff technology can be found in fashion. People who are always dropping their sunglasses may have invested in a pair of sunglasses with scratch resistant lenses—that is, it's impossible to scratch the glass, even if the glasses are dropped on an abrasive surface. This innovation is incredibly advantageous for people who are clumsy, but most shoppers don't know that this technology was originally developed by NASA. Scientists first created scratch resistant glass to help protect costly and crucial equipment from getting scratched in space, especially the helmet visors in space suits. However, sunglasses companies later realized that this technology could be profitable for their products, and they licensed the technology from NASA.

12. What is the main purpose of this article?
    a. To advise consumers to do more research before making a purchase
    b. To persuade readers to support NASA research
    c. To tell a narrative about the history of space technology
    d. To define and describe instances of spinoff technology

13. What is the organizational structure of this article?
    a. A general definition followed by more specific examples
    b. A general opinion followed by supporting evidence
    c. An important moment in history followed by chronological details
    d. A popular misconception followed by counterevidence

14. Why did NASA scientists research algae?
    a. They already knew algae was healthy for babies.
    b. They were interested in how to grow food in space.
    c. They were looking for ways to add health benefits to food.
    d. They hoped to use it to protect expensive research equipment.

15. What does the word "neurological" mean in the second paragraph?
    a. Related to the body
    b. Related to the brain
    c. Related to vitamins
    d. Related to technology

16. Why does the author mention space suit helmets?
    a. To give an example of astronaut fashion
    b. To explain where sunglasses got their shape
    c. To explain how astronauts protect their eyes
    d. To give an example of valuable space equipment

17. Which statement would the author probably NOT agree with?
    a. Consumers don't always know the history of the products they are buying.
    b. Sometimes new innovations have unexpected applications.
    c. It is difficult to make money from scientific research.
    d. Space equipment is often very expensive.

Questions 18-24 are based on the following passage:

People who argue that William Shakespeare is not responsible for the plays attributed to his name are known as anti-Stratfordians (from the name of Shakespeare's birthplace, Stratford-upon-Avon). The most common anti-Stratfordian claim is that William Shakespeare simply was not educated enough or from a high enough social class to have written plays overflowing with references to such a wide range of subjects like history, the classics, religion, and international culture. William Shakespeare was the son of a glove-maker, he only had a basic grade school education, and he never set foot outside of England—so how could he have produced plays of such sophistication and imagination? How could he have written in such detail about historical figures and events, or about different cultures and locations around Europe? According to anti-Stratfordians, the depth of knowledge contained in Shakespeare's plays suggests a well-traveled writer from a wealthy background with a university education, not a countryside writer like

Shakespeare. But in fact, there is not much substance to such speculation, and most anti-Stratfordian arguments can be refuted with a little background about Shakespeare's time and upbringing.

First of all, those who doubt Shakespeare's authorship often point to his common birth and brief education as stumbling blocks to his writerly genius. Although it is true that Shakespeare did not come from a noble class, his father was a very *successful* glove-maker and his mother was from a very wealthy land-owning family—so while Shakespeare may have had a country upbringing, he was certainly from a well-off family and would have been educated accordingly. Also, even though he did not attend university, grade school education in Shakespeare's time was actually quite rigorous and exposed students to classic drama through writers like Seneca and Ovid. It is not unreasonable to believe that Shakespeare received a very solid foundation in poetry and literature from his early schooling.

Next, anti-Stratfordians tend to question how Shakespeare could write so extensively about countries and cultures he had never visited before (for instance, several of his most famous works like *Romeo and Juliet* and *The Merchant of Venice* were set in Italy, on the opposite side of Europe!). But again, this criticism does not hold up under scrutiny. For one thing, Shakespeare was living in London, a bustling metropolis of international trade, the most populous city in England, and a political and cultural hub of Europe. In the daily crowds of people, Shakespeare would certainly have been able to meet travelers from other countries and hear firsthand accounts of life in their home country. And, in addition to the influx of information from world travelers, this was also the age of the printing press, a jump in technology that made it possible to print and circulate books much more easily than in the past. This also allowed for a freer flow of information across different countries, allowing people to read about life and ideas from throughout Europe. One needn't travel the continent in order to learn and write about its culture.

18. What is the main purpose of this article?
    a. To explain two sides of an argument and allow readers to choose which side they agree with
    b. To encourage readers to be skeptical about the authorship of famous poems and plays
    c. To give historical background about an important literary figure
    d. To criticize a theory by presenting counterevidence

19. Which sentence contains the author's thesis?
    a. People who argue that William Shakespeare is not responsible for the plays attributed to his name are known as anti-Stratfordians.
    b. But in fact, there is not much substance to such speculation, and most anti-Stratfordian arguments can be refuted with a little background about Shakespeare's time and upbringing.
    c. It is not unreasonable to believe that Shakespeare received a very solid foundation in poetry and literature from his early schooling.
    d. Next, anti-Stratfordians tend to question how Shakespeare could write so extensively about countries and cultures he had never visited before.

20. How does the author respond to the claim that Shakespeare was not well-educated because he did not attend university?
    a. By insisting upon Shakespeare's natural genius
    b. By explaining grade school curriculum in Shakespeare's time
    c. By comparing Shakespeare with other uneducated writers of his time
    d. By pointing out that Shakespeare's wealthy parents probably paid for private tutors

21. What does the word "bustling" in the third paragraph most nearly mean?
    a. Busy
    b. Foreign
    c. Expensive
    d. Undeveloped

22. What can be inferred from the article?
    a. Shakespeare's peers were jealous of his success and wanted to attack his reputation.
    b. Until recently, classic drama was only taught in universities.
    c. International travel was extremely rare in Shakespeare's time.
    d. In Shakespeare's time, glove-makers were not part of the upper class.

23. Why does the author mention *Romeo and Juliet*?
    a. It is Shakespeare's most famous play.
    b. It was inspired by Shakespeare's trip to Italy.
    c. It is an example of a play set outside of England.
    d. It was unpopular when Shakespeare first wrote it.

24. Which statement would the author probably agree with?
    a. It is possible to learn things from reading rather than from firsthand experience.
    b. If you want to be truly cultured, you need to travel the world.
    c. People never become successful without a university education.
    d. All of the world's great art comes from Italy.

Questions 25-28 refer to the following paragraph:

> Four score and seven years ago our fathers brought forth on this continent, a new nation, conceived in Liberty, and dedicated to the proposition that all men are created equal.
>
> Now we are engaged in a great civil war, testing whether that nation, or any nation so conceived and so dedicated, can long endure. We are met on a great battle-field of that war. We have come to dedicate a portion of that field, as a final resting place for those who here gave their lives that that nation might live. It is altogether fitting and proper that we should do this.
>
> But, in a larger sense, we cannot dedicate --- we cannot consecrate that we cannot hallow --- this ground. The brave men, living and dead, who struggled here, have consecrated it, far above our poor power to add or detract. The world will little note, nor long remember what we say here, but it can never forget what they did here. It is for us the living, rather, to be dedicated here to the unfinished work which they who fought here have thus far so nobly advanced. It is rather for us to be here dedicated to the great task remaining before us--- that from these honored dead we take increased devotion to that cause for which they gave the last full measure of devotion --- that we here highly resolve that these dead shall not have died in vain --

- that this nation, under God, shall have a new birth of freedom---and that government of the people, by the people, for the people, shall not perish from the earth.

Abraham Lincoln's Address Delivered at the Dedication of the Cemetery at Gettysburg, 1863

25. The best description for the phrase "Four score and seven years ago" is?
    a. A unit of measurement
    b. A period of time
    c. A literary movement
    d. A statement of political reform

26. Which war is Abraham Lincoln referring to in the following passage? "Now we are engaged in a great civil war, testing whether that nation, or any nation so conceived and so dedicated, can long endure."
    a. World War I
    b. The War of Spanish Succession
    c. World War II
    d. The American Civil War

27. What message is the author trying to convey through this address?
    a. The audience should perpetuate the ideals of freedom that the soldiers died fighting for.
    b. The audience should honor the dead by establishing an annual memorial service.
    c. The audience should form a militia that would overturn the current political structure.
    d. The audience should forget the lives that were lost and discredit the soldiers.

28. What is the effect of Lincoln's statement in the following passage? "But, in a larger sense, we cannot dedicate --- we cannot consecrate that we cannot hallow --- this ground. The brave men, living and dead, who struggled here, have consecrated it, far above our poor power to add or detract."
    a. His comparison emphasizes the great sacrifice of the soldiers who fought in the war.
    b. His comparison serves as a remainder of the inadequacies of his audience.
    c. His comparison serves as a catalyst for guilt and shame among audience members.
    d. His comparison attempts to illuminate the great differences between soldiers and civilians.

Question 29 is based on the following conversation between a scientist and a politician:

Scientist: Last year was the warmest ever recorded in the last 134 years. During that time period, the ten warmest years have all occurred since 2000. This correlates directly with the recent increases in carbon dioxide as large countries like China, India, and Brazil continue developing and industrializing. No longer do just a handful of countries burn massive amounts of carbon-based fossil fuels; it is quickly becoming the case throughout the whole world as technology and industry spread.

Politician: Yes, but there is no causal link between increases in carbon emissions and increasing temperatures. The link is tenuous and nothing close to certain. We need to wait for all of the data before drawing hasty conclusions. For all we know, the temperature increase could be entirely natural. I believe the temperatures also rose dramatically during the dinosaurs' time, and I do not think they were burning any fossil fuels back then.

29. What is one point on which the scientist and politician agree?
   a. Burning fossil fuels causes global temperatures to rise.
   b. Global temperatures are increasing.
   c. Countries must revisit their energy policies before it's too late.
   d. Earth's climate naturally goes through warming and cooling periods.

Questions 30–34 are based upon the following passage:

> Insects as a whole are preeminently creatures of the land and the air. This is shown not only by the possession of wings by a vast majority of the class, but by the mode of breathing to which reference has already been made, a system of branching air-tubes carrying atmospheric air with its combustion-supporting oxygen to all the insect's tissues. The air gains access to these tubes through a number of paired air-holes or spiracles, arranged segmentally in series.
>
> It is of great interest to find that, nevertheless, a number of insects spend much of their time under water. This is true of not a few in the perfect winged state, as for example aquatic beetles and water-bugs ('boatmen' and 'scorpions') which have some way of protecting their spiracles when submerged, and, possessing usually the power of flight, can pass on occasion from pond or stream to upper air. But it is advisable in connection with our present subject to dwell especially on some insects that remain continually under water till they are ready to undergo their final moult and attain the winged state, which they pass entirely in the air. The preparatory instars of such insects are aquatic; the adult instar is aerial. All may-flies, dragon-flies, and caddis-flies, many beetles and two-winged flies, and a few moths thus divide their life-story between the water and the air. For the present we confine attention to the Stone-flies, the May-flies, and the Dragon-flies, three well-known orders of insects respectively called by systematists the Plecoptera, the Ephemeroptera, and the Odonata.
>
> In the case of many insects that have aquatic larvae, the latter are provided with some arrangement for enabling them to reach atmospheric air through the surface-film of the water. But the larva of a stone-fly, a dragon-fly, or a may-fly is adapted more completely than these for aquatic life; it can, by means of gills of some kind, breathe the air dissolved in water.

This excerpt is from *The Life-Story of Insects* by Geo H. Carpenter

30. Which statement best details the central idea in this passage?
   a. It introduces certain insects that transition from water to air.
   b. It delves into entomology, especially where gills are concerned.
   c. It defines what constitutes insects' breathing.
   d. It invites readers to have a hand in the preservation of insects.

31. What is the purpose of the first paragraph in relation to the second paragraph?
   a. The first paragraph serves as a cause, and the second paragraph serves as an effect.
   b. The first paragraph serves as a contrast to the second.
   c. The first paragraph is a description for the argument in the second paragraph.
   d. The first and second paragraphs are merely presented in a sequence.

32. What does the following sentence most nearly mean?

The preparatory instars of such insects are aquatic; the adult instar is aerial.

a. The volume of water is necessary to prep the insect for transition rather than the volume of the air.
b. The abdomen of the insect is designed like a star in the water as well as the air.
c. The early stages in between periods of molting are acted out in the water, while the last stage is in the air.
d. These insects breathe first in the water through gills yet continue to use the same organs to breathe in the air.

33. Which of the statements reflect information that one could reasonably infer based on the author's tone?
a. The author's tone is persuasive and attempts to call the audience to action.
b. The author's tone is passionate due to excitement over the subject and personal narrative.
c. The author's tone is informative and exhibits interest in the subject of the study.
d. The author's tone is somber, depicting some anger at the state of insect larvae.

34. Which statement best describes stoneflies, mayflies, and dragonflies?
a. They are creatures of the land and the air.
b. They have a way of protecting their spiracles when submerged.
c. Their larvae can breathe the air dissolved in water through gills of some kind.
d. The preparatory instars of these insects are aerial.

Questions 35 and 36 refer to the passage below:

> I believe that this was the first moving line ever installed. The idea came in a general way from the overhead trolley that the Chicago packers use in dressing beef. We had previously assembled the fly-wheel magneto in the usual method. With one workman doing a complete job he could turn out from thirty-five to forty pieces in a nine-hour day, or about twenty minutes to an assembly. What he did alone was then spread into twenty-nine operations; that cut down the assembly time to thirteen minutes, ten seconds. Then we raised the height of the line eight inches—this was in 1914—and cut the time to seven minutes. Further experimenting with the speed that the work should move at cut the time down to five minutes. In short, the result is this: by the aid of scientific study one man is now able to do somewhat more than four did only a comparatively few years ago. That line established the efficiency of the method and we now use it everywhere. The assembling of the motor, formerly done by one man, is now divided into eighty-four operations—those men do the work that three times their number formerly did. In a short time we tried out the plan on the chassis.

Excerpt from *My Life and My Work* by Henry Ford, 1922

35. According to the passage, which one of the following best describes the primary economic benefit of this innovation?
   a. The innovation increased workers' ability to multi-task.
   b. The innovation decreased labor costs per worker.
   c. The innovation increased productivity in terms of both speed and quantity.
   d. The innovation decreased the size of the industrial workforce.

36. According to the passage, how did this new method of production improve over time?
   a. The method improved by adopting the exact practices of other industries.
   b. The method improved after it was applied to the chassis.
   c. The method improved by continually increasing the number of operations per product.
   d. The method improved progressively through experimentation.

Answer Explanations #2

Algebra and Functions

1. D: Finding the zeros for a function by factoring is done by setting the equation equal to zero, then completely factoring. Since there is a common x for each term in the provided equation, that should be factored out first. Then the quadratic that is left can be factored into two binomials, which are $(x + 1)(x - 4)$. Setting each factor equal to zero and solving for x yields three zeros.

2. D: Dividing rational expressions follows the same rule as dividing fractions. The division is changed to multiplication by the reciprocal of the second fraction. This turns the expression into:

$$\frac{5x^3}{3x^2y} \times \frac{3y^9}{25}$$

This can be simplified by finding common factors in the numerators and denominators of the two fractions.

$$\frac{x^3}{x^2y} \times \frac{y^9}{5}$$

Multiplying across creates:

$$\frac{x^3y^9}{5x^2y}$$

Simplifying leads to the final expression of:

$$\frac{xy^8}{5}$$

3. B: The table shows values that are increasing exponentially. The differences between the inputs are the same, while the differences in the outputs are changing by a factor of 2. The values in the table can be modeled by the equation $f(x) = 2^x$.

4. A: Using the trigonometric identity $\tan(\theta) = \frac{\sin(\theta)}{\cos(\theta)}$, the expression becomes $\frac{\sin\theta}{\cos\theta}\cos\theta$. The factors that are the same on the top and bottom cancel out, leaving the simplified expression $\sin\theta$.

5. C: The equation $x = 3$ is not a function because it does not pass the vertical line test. This test is made from the definition of a function, where each x-value must be mapped to one and only one y-value. This equation is a vertical line, so the x-value of 3 is mapped with an infinite number of y-values.

6. A: The function can be factored to identify the zeros. First, the term $3x$ is factored out to the front because each term contains $3x$. Then, the quadratic is factored into $(x + 3)(x - 2)$.

7. B: The first step is to use the quadratic formula on the first equation ($x^2 - x - 3 = 0$) to solve for x. In this case, a is 1, b is -1, and c is -3, yielding:

$$x = \frac{-b \pm \sqrt{b^2 - 4ac}}{2a}$$

$$x = \frac{1 \pm \sqrt{1 - 4 \times 1(-3)}}{2}$$

$$x = \frac{1}{2} \pm \frac{\sqrt{13}}{2}$$

Therefore, $x - \frac{1}{2}$, which is in our second equation, equals $\pm\frac{\sqrt{13}}{2}$. We are looking for $\left(x - \frac{1}{2}\right)^2$ though, so we square the $\pm\frac{\sqrt{13}}{2}$. Doing so causes the $\pm$ to cancel and we are left with:

$$\left(x - \frac{1}{2}\right)^2 = \left(\frac{\sqrt{13}}{2}\right)^2 = \frac{13}{4}$$

8. B: The independent variable's coordinate at the vertex of a parabola (which is the highest point when the coefficient of the squared independent variable is negative) is given by $x = -\frac{b}{2a}$. Substitute and solve for x to get:

$$x = -\frac{4}{2(-16)} = \frac{1}{8}$$

Using this value of x, the maximum height of the ball (y), can be calculated. Substituting x into the equation yields:

$$h(t) = -16\left(\frac{1}{8}\right)^2 + 4\frac{1}{8} + 6 = 6.25$$

9. B: The domain is all possible input values, or *x*-values. For this equation, the domain is every number greater than or equal to zero. There are no negative numbers in the domain because taking the square root of a negative number results in an imaginary number.

10. D: The inverse of a function is found by following these steps:

1. Change f(x) to y.

2. Switch the x and y in the equation.

3. Solve for y. In the given equation, solving for y is done by adding 5 to both sides, then dividing both sides by 3.

This answer can be checked on the graph by verifying the lines are reflected over $y = x$.

11. A: The equation is *even* because $f(-x) = f(x)$. Plugging in a negative value will result in the same answer as when plugging in the positive of that same value. For example:

$$f(-2) = \frac{1}{2}(-2)^4 + 2(-2)^2 - 6 = 8 + 8 - 6 = 10$$

This function yields the same value as:

$$f(2) = \frac{1}{2}(2)^4 + 2(2)^2 - 6 = 8 + 8 - 6 = 10$$

12. D: Each value can be substituted into each equation. Choice *A* can be eliminated, since $4^2 + 16 = 32$. Choice *B* can be eliminated, since $4^2 + 4 \times 4 - 4 = 28$. Choice *C* can be eliminated, since $4^2 - 2 \times 4 - 2 = 6$. But, plugging in either value into $x^2 - 16$ gives:

$$(\pm 4)^2 - 16 = 16 - 16 = 0$$

13. C: If $y = f^{-1}(6)$ then *y* must satisfy $f(y) = 6$. Substituting and solving for y yields $4y + 2 = 6$, then $4y = 4$, and $y = 1$.

14. B: The slope will be given by:

$$m = \frac{y_2 - y_1}{x_2 - x_1}$$

$$m = \frac{1 - 0}{2 - 0} = \frac{1}{2}$$

The y-intercept will be 0 since it passes through the origin. Using slope-intercept form, the equation for this line is:

$$y = \frac{1}{2}x$$

15. B: The y-intercept of an equation is found where the x -value is zero. Plugging zero into the equation for x, the first two terms cancel out, leaving -4.

16. B: Start by squaring both sides to get $1 + x = 16$. Then subtract 1 from both sides to get $x = 15$.

17. C: Multiply both sides by *x* to get $x + 2 = 2x$, which simplifies to $-x = -2$, or *x* = 2.

18. B: $\frac{2}{a}$ must be subtracted from both sides, with a result of $\frac{1}{x} = \frac{2}{b} - \frac{2}{a}$. The reciprocal of both sides needs to be taken, but the right-hand side needs to be written as a single fraction in order to do that. Since the two fractions on the right have denominators that are not equal, a common denominator of *ab* is needed. This leaves $\frac{1}{x} = \frac{2a}{ab} - \frac{2b}{ab} = \frac{2(a-b)}{ab}$. Taking the reciprocals, which can be done since *b* – *a* is not zero, with a result of $x = \frac{ab}{2(a-b)}$.

19. B: Recall that to compose functions, replace the *x* in the expression for *g* with the expression for *f* everywhere there is x. So:

$$g(f(x)) = \frac{f(x) - 1}{4} = \frac{2x + 1 - 1}{4} = \frac{2x}{4} = \frac{x}{2}$$

20. B: Here, *f* is an exponential function whose base is less than 1. In this function, *f* is always decreasing. This means that when *a* is less than *b*, $f(a) > f(b)$.

21. B: From the slope-intercept form, $y = mx + b$, it is known that *b* is the *y*-intercept, which is 1. Compute the slope as $\frac{2-1}{1-0} = 1$, so the equation is $y = x + 1$.

22. A: This has the form $t^2 - y^2$, with $t = x^2$ and $y = 4$. It's also known that $t^2 - y^2 = (t + y)(t - y)$, and substituting the values for *t* and *y* into the right-hand side gives $(x^2 - 4)(x^2 + 4)$.

23. D: Finding the slope of the line tangent to the given function involves taking the derivative twice. The first derivative gives the line tangent to the graph. The second derivative finds the slope of that line. The line tangent to the graph has an equation $y' = 3x^2$. The slope of this line at $x = 2$ is found by the second derivative, $y = 6x$, or $y = 6(2) = 12$.

24. C: A function is continuous over its domain. This function is a quotient of two functions. The function in the numerator has a domain of $[2, \infty)$ because the radicand has to be non-negative. The function in the denominator has a domain of $(-\infty, 2) \cup (2, \infty)$ because it cannot be equal to zero. The intersection of these two domains, which is the domain of the entire function, is $(2, \infty)$.

25. C: Apply the power rule, to get $2 \times 3x^{3-1} = 6x^2$.

26. D: The values for x and y should be plugged into the equation to find the correct answer.

$$3.2(2.6)(5.3) - 4.1(5.3) = 22.366$$

27. B: First, subtract 9 from both sides to isolate the radical. Then, cube each side of the equation to obtain:

$$2x + 11 = 27$$

Subtract 11 from both sides, and then divide by 2. The result is $x = 8$. Plug 8 back into the original equation to check the answer:

$$\sqrt[3]{16 + 11} + 9 = 12$$

$$\sqrt[3]{27} + 9 = 12$$

$$3 + 9 = 12$$

28. B: The system can be solved using substitution. Solve the second equation for *y*, resulting in:

$$y = 1 - 2x$$

Plugging this into the first equation results in the quadratic equation:

$$x^2 - 2x + 1 = 4$$

In standard form, this equation is equivalent to $x^2 - 2x - 3 = 0$ and in factored form is:

$$(x-3)(x+1) = 0$$

Its solutions are $x = 3$ and $x = -1$. Plugging these values into the second equation results in $y = -5$ and $y = 3$, respectively. Therefore, the solutions are the ordered pairs $(-1, 3)$ and $(3, -5)$.

29. B: The function presented is being evaluated for $x + 1$; therefore, $x + 1$ must be substituted into the original function as follows:

$$f(x+1) = (x+1)^2 - 3(x+1) + 17$$

The squared portion of the function becomes $x^2 + 2x + 1$, and distributing the -3 results in:

$$f(x+1) = x^2 + 2x + 1 - 3x - 3 + 17$$

Combining like terms results in:

$$x^2 - x + 15$$

30. C: Finding the product means distributing one polynomial to the other so that each term in the first is multiplied by each term in the second. Then, like terms can be collected. Multiplying the factors yields the expression:

$$x^3 + 5x^2 - 6x + 2x^2 + 10x - 12$$

Collecting like terms means adding the x^2 terms and adding the x-terms. The final answer after simplifying the expression is:

$$x^3 + 7x^2 + 4x - 12$$

31. A: Finding the roots means finding the values of *x* when *y* is zero. The quadratic formula could be used, but in this case, it is possible to factor by hand, since the numbers -1 and 2 add to 1 and multiply to -2. So, factor $x^2 + x - 2 = (x-1)(x+2) = 0$, then set each factor equal to zero. Solving for each value gives the values *x* = 1 and *x* = -2.

32. C: To find the *y*-intercept, substitute zero for x, which gives us:

$$y = 0^{\frac{5}{3}} + (0-3)(0+1) = 0 + (-3)(1) = -3$$

33. A: Simplify this to:

$$(4x^2y^4)^{\frac{3}{2}} = 4^{\frac{3}{2}}(x^2)^{\frac{3}{2}}(y^4)^{\frac{3}{2}}$$

$$4^{\frac{3}{2}} = (\sqrt{4})^3 = 2^3 = 8$$

For the other, recall that the exponents must be multiplied; this yields:

$$8x^{2\cdot\frac{3}{2}}y^{4\cdot\frac{3}{2}} = 8x^3y^6$$

Reading Comprehension

1. D: It emphasizes Mr. Utterson's anguish in failing to identify Hyde's whereabouts. Context clues indicate that Choice *D* is correct because the passage provides great detail of Mr. Utterson's feelings about locating Hyde. Choice *A* does not fit because there is no mention of Mr. Lanyon's mental state. Choice *B* is incorrect; although the text does make mention of bells, Choice *B* is not the *best* answer overall. Choice *C* is incorrect because the passage clearly states that Mr. Utterson was determined, not unsure.

2. A: In the city. The word *city* appears in the passage several times, thus establishing the location for the reader.

3. B: It scares children. The passage states that the Juggernaut causes the children to scream. Choices *A* and *D* don't apply because the text doesn't mention either of these instances specifically. Choice *C* is incorrect because there is nothing in the text that mentions space travel.

4. B: To constantly visit. The mention of *morning*, *noon*, and *night* make it clear that the word *haunt* refers to frequent appearances at various times. Choice *A* doesn't work because the text makes no mention of levitating. Choices *C* and *D* are not correct because the text makes mention of Mr. Utterson's anguish and disheartenment because of his failure to find Hyde but does not make mention of Mr. Utterson's feelings negatively affecting anyone else.

5. D: This is an example of alliteration. Choice *D* is the correct answer because of the repetition of the *L*-words. Hyperbole is an exaggeration, so Choice *A* doesn't work. No comparison is being made, so no simile or juxtaposition is being used, thus eliminating Choices *B* and *C*.

6. D: The speaker intends to continue to look for Hyde. Choices *A* and *B* are not possible answers because the text doesn't refer to any name changes or an identity crisis, despite Mr. Utterson's extreme obsession with finding Hyde. The text also makes no mention of a mistaken identity when referring to Hyde, so Choice *C* is also incorrect.

7. B: Readers should carefully focus their attention on the beginning of the passage to answer this series of questions. Even though the sentences may be worded a bit differently, all but one statement is true. It presents a false idea that descriptive details are not necessary until the climax of the story. Even if one does not read the passage, he or she probably knows that all good writing begins with descriptive details to develop the main theme the writer intends for the narrative.

8. B: To suggest that a ten-minute play is accessible does not imply any timeline, nor does the passage mention how long a playwright spends with revisions and rewrites. So, Choice *A* is incorrect. Choice *B* is correct because of the opening statement that reads, "Learning how to write a ten-minute play may seem like a monumental task at first; but, if you follow a simple creative writing strategy, similar to writing a narrative story, you will be able to write a successful drama." None of the remaining choices are supported by points in the passage.

9. D: Note that the only element not mentioned in the passage is the style feature that is part of a narrative writer's tool kit. It is not to say that ten-minute plays do not have style. The correct answer denotes only that the element of style was not illustrated in this particular passage.

10. C: This choice allows room for the fact that not all people who attempt to write a play will find it easy. If the writer follows the basic principles of narrative writing described in the passage, however, writing a play does not have to be an excruciating experience. None of the other options can be supported by points from the passage.

11. C: We are looking for an inference—a conclusion that is reached on the basis of evidence and reasoning—from the passage that will likely explain why the famous children's author did not achieve her usual success with the new genre (despite the book's acclaim). Choice *A* is wrong because the statement is false according to the passage. Choice *B* is wrong because, although the passage says the author has a graduate degree on the subject, it would be an unrealistic leap to infer that she is the foremost expert on Antebellum America. Choice *D* is wrong because there is nothing in the passage to lead us to infer that people generally prefer a children's series to historical fiction. In contrast, Choice *C* can be logically inferred since the passage speaks of the great success of the children's series and the declaration that the fame of the author's name causes the children's books to "fly off the shelves." Thus, she did not receive any bump from her name since she published the historical novel under a pseudonym, which makes Choice *C* correct.

12. D: To define and describe instances of spinoff technology. This is an example of a purpose question—*why* did the author write this? The article contains facts, definitions, and other objective information without telling a story or arguing an opinion. In this case, the purpose of the article is to inform the reader. Choices A and B are incorrect because they argue for an opinion or present a position. Choice C is incorrect because the focus of the article is spinoff technology, not the history of space technology.

13. B: A general opinion followed by supporting evidence. This organization question asks readers to analyze the structure of the essay. The topic of the essay is about spinoff technology, and the thesis statement at the end of the first paragraph offers the opinion, "Spinoff technology proves that it is worthwhile to invest in science research because it could enrich people's lives in unexpected ways." The next two paragraphs provide evidence to support this opinion. Choice A is the second-best option because the first paragraph gives a general definition of spinoff technology, while the following two paragraphs offer more detailed examples to help illustrate this idea. However, it is not the best answer because the main idea of the essay is that spinoff technology enriches people's lives in unexpected ways. Choice C is incorrect because the essay does not provide details of any specific moment in history. Choice D is incorrect because the essay does not discuss a popular misconception.

14. C: They were looking for ways to add health benefits to food. This reading comprehension question can be answered based on the second paragraph—scientists were concerned about astronauts' nutrition and began researching useful nutritional supplements. Choice *A* in particular is not true because it reverses the order of discovery (first NASA identified algae for astronaut use, and then it was further developed for use in baby food). Choices *B* and *D* are not uses of algae discussed in the article.

15. B: Even for readers who have never encountered the word "neurological" before, the passage does provide context clues. The sentence following the statement about neurological benefits says algae has "potential to boost brain health." From this context, readers should be able to infer that "neurological" is related to the brain.

16. D: To give an example of valuable space equipment. This purpose question requires readers to understand the relevance of the given detail. In this case, the author mentions "costly and crucial equipment" before mentioning space suit visors, which are given as an example of something that is very valuable. *A* is not correct because fashion is only related to sunglasses, not to NASA equipment. *B* can be eliminated because it is simply not mentioned in the passage. While *C* seems like it could be a true statement, it is also not relevant to what is being explained by the author.

17. C: It is difficult to make money from scientific research. The article gives several examples of how businesses have been able to capitalize on NASA research, so it is unlikely that the author would agree with this statement. Evidence for the other answer choices can be found in the article: In Choice *A*, the author mentions that "many consumers are unaware that products they are buying are based on NASA research." Choice *B* is a general definition of spinoff technology. Choice *D* is mentioned in the final paragraph.

18. D: To criticize a theory by presenting counterevidence. The author mentions anti-Stratfordian arguments in the first paragraph, but then goes on to debunk these theories with more facts about Shakespeare's life in the second and third paragraphs. *A* is not correct because, while the author does present arguments from both sides, the author is far from unbiased; in fact, the author clearly disagrees with anti-Stratfordians. *B* is also not correct because it is more closely aligned to the beliefs of anti-Stratfordians, whom the author disagrees with. *C* can be eliminated because, while it is true that the author gives historical background, the main purpose of the article is using that information to disprove a theory.

19. B: But in fact, there is not much substance to such speculation, and most anti-Stratfordian arguments can be refuted with a little background about Shakespeare's time and upbringing. The thesis is a statement that contains the author's topic and main idea. As seen in question 7, the main purpose of this article is to use historical evidence to provide counterarguments to anti-Stratfordians. *A* is simply a definition; *C* is a supporting detail, not a main idea; and *D* represents an idea of anti-Stratfordians, not the author's opinion.

20. B: By explaining grade school curriculum in Shakespeare's time. This question asks readers to refer to the organizational structure of the article and demonstrate understanding of how the author provides details to support their argument. This particular detail can be found in the second paragraph: "even though he did not attend university, grade school education in Shakespeare's time was actually quite rigorous."

21. A: Busy. This is a vocabulary question that can be answered using context clues. Other sentences in the paragraph describe London as "the most populous city in England" filled with "crowds of people," giving an image of a busy city full of people. *B* is not correct because London was in Shakespeare's home country, not a foreign one. *C* is not mentioned in the passage. *D* is not a good answer choice because the passage describes how London was a popular and important city, probably not an underdeveloped one.

22. D: In Shakespeare's time, glove-makers were not part of the upper class. Anti-Stratfordians doubt Shakespeare's ability because he was not from the upper class; his father was a glove-maker; therefore, in at least this instance, glove-makers were not included in the upper class (this is an example of inductive reasoning, or using two specific pieces of information to draw a more general conclusion).

23. C: It is an example of a play set outside of England. This detail comes from the third paragraph, where the author responds to skeptics who claim that Shakespeare wrote too much about places he never visited, so *Romeo and Juliet* is mentioned as a famous example of a play with a foreign setting. In order to answer this question, readers need to understand the author's main purpose in the third paragraph and how the author uses details to support this purpose. *A* and *D* are not mentioned in the passage, and *B* is clearly not true because the passage mentions more than once that Shakespeare never left England.

24. A: It is possible to learn things from reading rather than from firsthand experience. This inference can be made from the final paragraph, where the author refutes anti-Stratfordian skepticism by pointing out that books about life in Europe could easily circulate throughout London. From this statement, readers can conclude that the author believes it is possible that Shakespeare learned about European culture from books, rather than visiting the continent on his own. *B* is not true because the author believes that Shakespeare contributed to English literature without traveling extensively. Similarly, *C* is not a good answer because the author explains how Shakespeare got his education without university. *D* can also be eliminated because the author describes Shakespeare's genius and clearly Shakespeare is not from Italy.

25. B: A period of time. "Four score and seven years ago" is the equivalent of eighty-seven years, because the word "score" means "twenty." *A* and *C* are incorrect because the context for describing a unit of measurement or a literary movement is lacking. *D* is incorrect because although Lincoln's speech is a cornerstone in political rhetoric, the phrase "Four score and seven years ago" is better narrowed to a period of time.

26. D: Abraham Lincoln is the former president of the United States, so the correct answer is *D*, "The American Civil War." Though the U.S. was involved in World War I and II, *A* and *C* are incorrect because a civil war specifically means citizens fighting within the same country. *B* is incorrect, as "The War of Spanish Succession" involved Spain, Italy, Germany, and Holland, and not the United States.

27. A: The speech calls on the audience to consider the soldiers who died on the battlefield as ideas to perpetuate freedom so that their deaths would not be in vain. *B* is incorrect because, although they are there to "dedicate a portion of that field," there is no mention in the text of an annual memorial service. *C* is incorrect because there is no charged language in the text, only reverence for the dead. *D* is incorrect because "forget[ting] the lives that were lost" is the opposite of what Lincoln is suggesting.

28. A: Choice A is correct because Lincoln's intention was to memorialize the soldiers who had fallen as a result of war as well as celebrate those who had put their lives in danger for the sake of their country. Choices B and C are incorrect because Lincoln's speech was supposed to foster a sense of pride among the members of the audience while connecting them to the soldiers' experiences. Choice D is incorrect because Lincoln does not a distinction between soldiers and civilians but rather pointing his audience toward the sacrifices made by the soldiers on the battlefield at Gettysburg.

29. B: The scientist and politician largely disagree, but the question asks for a point where the two are in agreement. The politician would not concur that burning fossil fuels causes global temperatures to rise; thus, Choice *A* is wrong. The politician also would not agree with Choice *C* suggesting that countries must revisit their energy policies. By inference from the given information, the scientist would likely not concur that earth's climate naturally goes through warming and cooling cycles; so Choice *D* is incorrect. However, both the scientist and politician would agree that global temperatures are increasing. The reason for this is in dispute. The politician thinks it is part of the earth's natural cycle; the scientist thinks it is from the burning of fossil fuels. However, both acknowledge an increase, so Choice *B* is the correct answer.

30. A: It introduces certain insects that transition from water to air. Choice *B* is incorrect because although the passage talks about gills, it is not the central idea of the passage. Choices *C* and *D* are incorrect because the passage does not "define" or "invite," but only serves as an introduction to stoneflies, dragonflies, and mayflies and their transition from water to air.

31. B: The first paragraph serves as a contrast to the second. Notice how the first paragraph goes into detail describing how insects are able to breathe air. The second paragraph acts as a contrast to the first by stating "[i]t is of great interest to find that, nevertheless, a number of insects spend much of their time under water." Watch for transition words such as "nevertheless" to help find what type of passage you're dealing with.

32: C: *Instars* are the phases between two periods of molting, and the text explains when these transitions occur. The preparatory stages are acted out in the water while the last stage is in the air. Choices *A*, *B*, and *D* are all incorrect.

33. C: The author's tone is informative and exhibits interest in the subject of the study. Overall, the author presents us with information on the subject. One moment where personal interest is depicted is when the author states, "It is of great interest to find that, nevertheless, a number of insects spend much of their time under water."

34. C: Their larva can breathe the air dissolved in water through gills of some kind. This is stated in the last paragraph. Choice *A* is incorrect because the text mentions this in a general way at the beginning of the passage concerning "insects as a whole." Choice *B* is incorrect because this is stated of beetles and water-bugs, and not the insects in question. Choice *D* is incorrect because this is the opposite of what the text says of instars.

35. C: The innovation's primary economic benefit was to increase productivity in terms of both speed and quality. The passage contains several examples of how the assembly increased the production of fly-wheel magnetos and motors. For example, at the end of the passage, Ford claims that the assembly line tripled the productivity for motors. Thus, Choice *C* is the correct answer. The innovation is that each worker is assigned one single operation to be completed on every product, which is the opposite of multi-tasking. So, Choice *A* is incorrect. Although the innovation might have decreased labor costs by standardizing tasks, the passage doesn't reference labor costs. Therefore, Choice *B* is incorrect. Choice *D* is the second best answer choice. Ford mentions that men can perform three times the amount of work, but it's unclear whether this means the workforce decreased. In other words, the workforce could've remained the same or even increased to support mass production. As such, Choice *D* is incorrect.

36. D: The method improved progressively through experimentation. Ford describes how he first got the idea from the overhead trolley used by Chicago beef packers and then they later elevated the height of the assembly line. In addition, the passage explicitly references "experimenting with the speed" of line and making use of "scientific study." Thus, Choice *D* is the correct answer. Choice *A* is the second best answer choice because the Chicago beef packing industry influenced Ford. However, Ford claims it was only loosely based on the beef industry's overhead trolley, and he repeatedly describes experimenting with the height and speed. So, Choice *A* is incorrect. The passage ends with Ford stating his intention to test the new method on a chassis, which is the automobile's frame. As such, the chassis didn't improve the method as described in the passage, so Choice *B* is incorrect. Choice *C* is incorrect because the increased number of operations was a consequence of Ford's experimentation; the method didn't improve simply because the number of operations increased. So, Choice *C* is incorrect.

Practice Test #3

Algebra and Functions

1. Which graph will be a line parallel to the graph of $y = 3x - 2$?
   a. $6x - 2y = -2$
   b. $4x - y = -4$
   c. $3y = x - 2$
   d. $2x - 2y = 2$

2. A company invests $50,000 in a building where they can produce saws. If the cost of producing one saw is $40, then which function expresses the amount of money the company pays? The variable *y* is the money paid and *x* is the number of saws produced.
   a. $y = 50{,}000x + 40$
   b. $y + 40 = x - 50{,}000$
   c. $y = 40x - 50{,}000$
   d. $y = 40x + 50{,}000$

3. If $3x = 6y = -2z = 24$, then what does $4xy + z$ equal?
   a. 116
   b. 130
   c. 84
   d. 108

4. Which inequality represents the following number line?

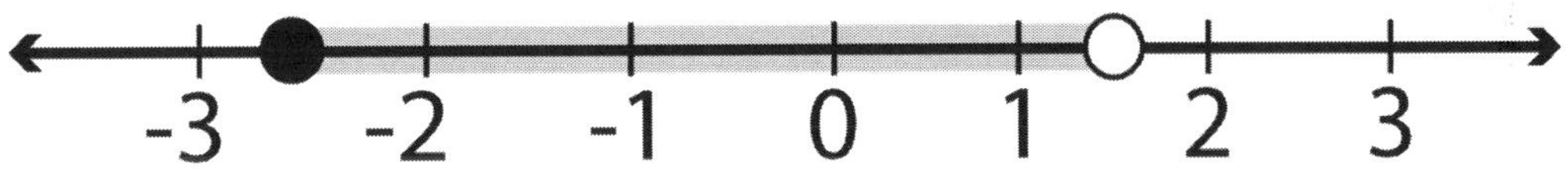

   a. $-\frac{5}{2} \leq x < \frac{3}{2}$
   b. $-\frac{7}{2} \leq x < \frac{5}{2}$
   c. $-\frac{5}{2} < x \leq \frac{3}{2}$
   d. $\frac{5}{2} < x \leq -\frac{3}{2}$

5. What is the equation of a circle whose center is (0, 0) and whole radius is 5?
   a. $(x-5)^2 + (y-5)^2 = 25$
   b. $(x)^2 + (y)^2 = 5$
   c. $(x)^2 + (y)^2 = 25$
   d. $(x+5)^2 + (y+5)^2 = 25$

6. Which of the ordered pairs below is a solution to the following system of inequalities?

$$y > 2x - 3$$
$$y < -4x + 8$$

a. $(4, 5)$
b. $(-3, -2)$
c. $(3, -1)$
d. $(5, 2)$

7. Which equation best represents the scatterplot below?

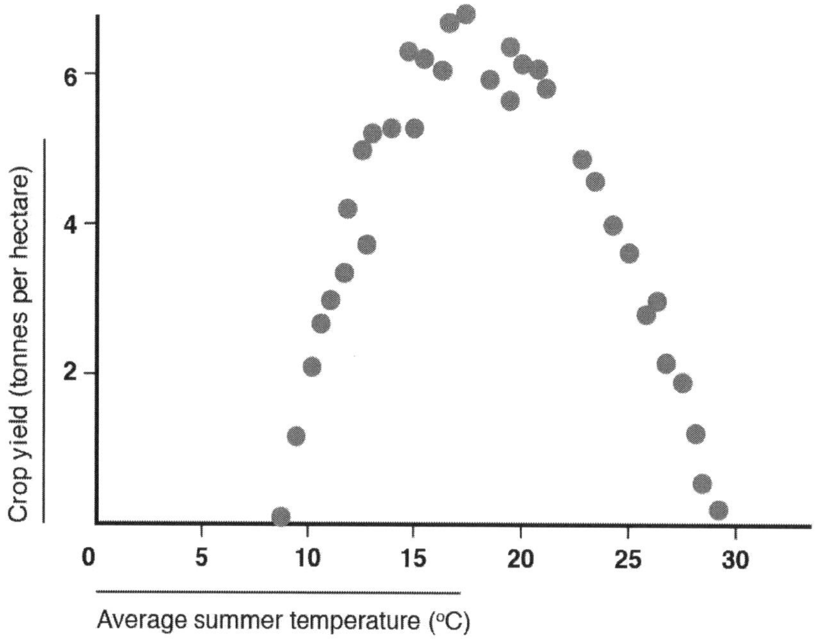

a. $y = 3x - 4$
b. $y = 2x^2 + 7x - 9$
c. $y = (3)(4^x)$
d. $y = -\frac{1}{14}x^2 + 2x - 8$

8. If $n = 2^2$, and $m = n^2$, then m^n equals?
a. 2^{12}
b. 2^{10}
c. 2^{18}
d. 2^{16}

9. The graph of the function $f(x) = |x+3| - 4$ is graphed on the coordinate plane below.

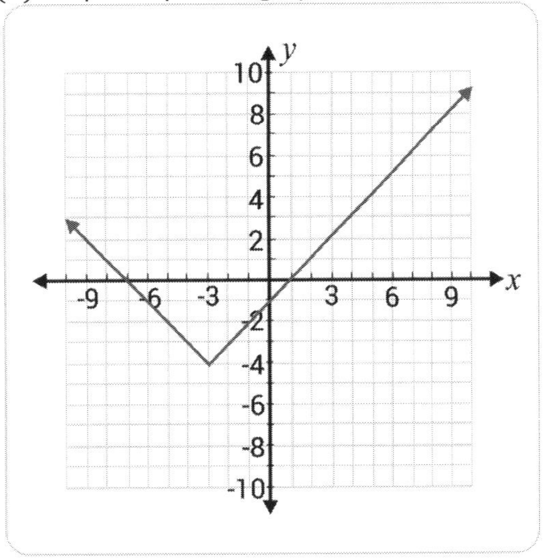

For which of the following functions does the graph of $g(x)$ intersect the function $f(x)$ exactly two times?

a. $g(x) = x - 4$
b. $g(x) = -x$
c. $g(x) = x + 2$
d. $g(x) = \frac{x}{2}$

10. If h is a multiple of 5, which of the following must also be multiples of 5?

a. $5h - 3$
b. $4h + 1$
c. $10h + 20$
d. $h^3 + 6$

11. Of the given sets of coordinates below, which ones lie on the line that is perpendicular to $y = 2x - 3$ and passes through the point $(0, 5)$?

a. $(-6, 10)$
b. $(-2, 7)$
c. $(2, 6)$
d. $(4, 3)$

12. Which of the following is the result of simplifying the expression:

$$\frac{4a^{-1}b^3}{a^4b^{-2}} \times \frac{3a}{b}$$

a. $12a^3b^5$

b. $12\frac{b^4}{a^4}$

c. $\frac{12}{a^4}$

d. $7\frac{b^4}{a}$

13. Write the expression for three times the sum of twice a number and one, minus 6.
  a. $2x + 1 - 6$
  b. $3x + 1 - 6$
  c. $3(x + 1) - 6$
  d. $3(2x + 1) - 6$

14. On Monday, Robert mopped the floor in 4 hours. On Tuesday, he did it in 3 hours. If on Monday, his average rate of mopping was *p* sq. ft. per hour, what was his average rate on Tuesday?
  a. $\frac{4}{3}p$ sq. ft. per hour
  b. $\frac{3}{4}p$ sq. ft. per hour
  c. $\frac{5}{4}p$ sq. ft. per hour
  d. $p + 1$ sq. ft. per hour

15. The phone bill is calculated each month using the equation $c = 50g + 75$. The cost of the phone bill per month is represented by c, and g represents the gigabytes of data used that month. What is the value and interpretation of the slope of this equation?
  a. 75 dollars per day
  b. 75 gigabytes per day
  c. 50 dollars per day
  d. 50 dollars per gigabyte

16. For the following similar triangles, what are the values of x and y (rounded to one decimal place)?

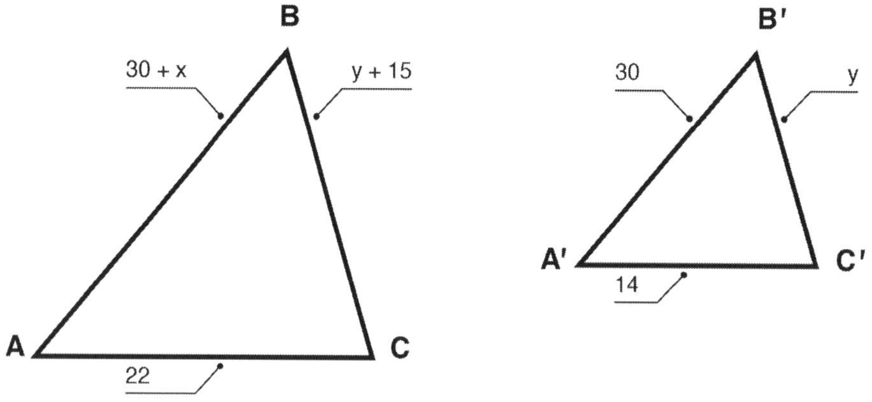

  a. $x = 16.5, y = 25.1$
  b. $x = 19.5, y = 24.1$
  c. $x = 17.1, y = 26.3$
  d. $x = 26.3, y = 17.1$

17. Solve for x, if $x^2 - 2x - 8 = 0$.

a. $2 \pm \frac{\sqrt{30}}{2}$
b. $2 \pm 4\sqrt{2}$
c. 1 ± 3
d. $4 \pm \sqrt{2}$

18. Which of the following is a factor of both $x^2 + 4x + 4$ and $x^2 - x - 6$?

a. $x - 3$
b. $x + 2$
c. $x - 2$
d. $x + 3$

19. What is the solution to the following system of equations?

$$x^2 - 2x + y = 8$$

$$x - y = -2$$

a. $(-2, 3)$
b. There is no solution.
c. $(-2, 0)\ (1, 3)$
d. $(-2, 0)\ (3, 5)$

20. What's the midpoint of a line segment with endpoints $(-1, 2)$ and $(3, -6)$?

a. $(1, 2)$
b. $(1, 0)$
c. $(-1, 2)$
d. $(1, -2)$

21. A sample data set contains the following values: 1, 3, 5, 7. What's the standard deviation of the set?

a. 2.58
b. 4
c. 6.23
d. 1.1

22. A line goes through the point $(-4, 0)$ and the point $(0, 2)$. What is the slope of the line?

a. 2
b. 4
c. $\frac{3}{2}$
d. $\frac{1}{2}$

23. Six people apply to work for Janice's company, but she only needs four workers. How many different groups of four employees can Janice choose?

a. 6
b. 10
c. 15
d. 36

24. $2x(3x+1)-5(3x+1)=$
   a. $10x(3x+1)$
   b. $10x^2(3x+1)$
   c. $(2x-5)(3x+1)$
   d. $(2x+1)(3x-5)$

25. For which real numbers *x* is $-3x^2+x-8>0$?
   a. All real numbers *x*
   b. $-2\sqrt{\frac{2}{3}}<x<2\sqrt{\frac{2}{3}}$
   c. $1-2\sqrt{\frac{2}{3}}<x<1+2\sqrt{\frac{2}{3}}$
   d. For no real numbers *x*

26. A root of x^2-2x-2 is
   a. $1+\sqrt{3}$
   b. $1+2\sqrt{2}$
   c. $2+2\sqrt{3}$
   d. $2-2\sqrt{3}$

27. In the *xy*-plane, the graph of $y=x^2+2$ and the circle with center $(0,1)$ and radius 1 have how many points of intersection?
   a. 0
   b. 1
   c. 2
   d. 3

28. What are the polynomial roots of x^2+x-2?
   a. 1 and -2
   b. -1 and 2
   c. 2 and -2
   d. 9 and 13

29. A farmer owns two (non-adjacent) square plots of land, which he wishes to fence. The area of one is 1,000 square feet, while the area of the other is 10 square feet. How much fencing does he need, in feet?
   a. 44
   b. $40\sqrt{10}$
   c. $440\sqrt{10}$
   d. $44\sqrt{10}$

30. How many different ways can we order the letters a, b, and c?
   a. 3
   b. 6
   c. 9
   d. 12

31. The sequence $\{a_n\}$ is defined by the relation $a_{n+1} = 3a_n - 1, a_1 = 1$. Find a_3.
   a. 2
   b. 4
   c. 5
   d. 15

32. What is the next number in the following series: $1, 3, 6, 10, 15, 21, \ldots$?
   a. 26
   b. 27
   c. 28
   d. 29

33. Carey bought 184 pounds of fertilizer to use on her lawn. Each segment of her lawn required $11\frac{1}{2}$ pounds of fertilizer to do a sufficient job. If a student were asked to determine how many segments could be fertilized with the amount purchased, what operation would be necessary to solve this problem?
   a. Multiplication
   b. Division
   c. Addition
   d. Subtraction

Reading Comprehension

Question 1 is based on the following passage:

Annabelle Rice started having trouble sleeping. Her biological clock was suddenly amiss and she began to lead a nocturnal schedule. She thought her insomnia was due to spending nights writing a horror story, but then she realized that even the idea of going outside into the bright world scared her to bits. She concluded she was now suffering from <u>heliophobia</u>.

1. Which of the following most accurately describes the meaning of the underlined word in the sentence above?
   a. Fear of dreams
   b. Fear of sunlight
   c. Fear of strangers
   d. Anxiety spectrum disorder

Questions 2-4 are based on the following passage:

George Washington emerged out of the American Revolution as an unlikely champion of liberty. On June 14, 1775, the Second Continental Congress created the Continental Army, and John Adams, serving in the Congress, nominated Washington to be its first commander. Washington fought under the British during the French and Indian War, and his experience and prestige proved instrumental to the American war effort. Washington provided invaluable leadership, training, and strategy during the Revolutionary War. He emerged from the war as the embodiment of liberty and freedom from tyranny.

After vanquishing the heavily favored British forces, Washington could have pronounced himself as the autocratic leader of the former colonies without any opposition, but he famously refused and returned to his Mount Vernon plantation. His restraint proved his commitment to the fledgling state's republicanism. Washington was later unanimously elected as the first American president. But it is Washington's farewell address that cemented his legacy as a visionary worthy of study.

In 1796, President Washington issued his farewell address by public letter. Washington enlisted his good friend, Alexander Hamilton, in drafting his most famous address. The letter expressed Washington's faith in the Constitution and rule of law. He encouraged his fellow Americans to put aside partisan differences and establish a national union. Washington warned Americans against meddling in foreign affairs and entering military alliances. Additionally, he stated his opposition to national political parties, which he considered partisan and counterproductive.

Americans would be wise to remember Washington's farewell, especially during presidential elections when politics hits a fever pitch. They might want to question the political institutions that were not planned by the Founding Fathers, such as the nomination process and political parties themselves.

2. Which of the following statements is logically based on the information contained in the passage above?
   a. George Washington's background as a wealthy landholder directly led to his faith in equality, liberty, and democracy.
   b. George Washington would have opposed America's involvement in the Second World War.
   c. George Washington would not have been able to write as great a farewell address without the assistance of Alexander Hamilton.
   d. George Washington would probably not approve of modern political parties.

3. Which of the following statements is the best description of the author's purpose in writing this passage about George Washington?
   a. To inform American voters about a Founding Father's sage advice on a contemporary issue and explain its applicability to modern times
   b. To introduce George Washington to readers as a historical figure worthy of study
   c. To note that George Washington was more than a famous military hero
   d. To convince readers that George Washington is a hero of republicanism and liberty

4. In which of the following materials would the author be the most likely to include this passage?
   a. A history textbook
   b. An obituary
   c. A fictional story
   d. A newspaper editorial

The following exchange occurred after the Baseball Coach's team suffered a heartbreaking loss in the final inning.

Reporter: The team clearly did not rise to the challenge. I'm sure that getting zero hits in twenty at-bats with runners in scoring position hurt the team's chances at winning the game. What are your thoughts on this devastating loss?

Baseball Coach: Hitting with runners in scoring position was not the reason we lost this game. We made numerous errors in the field, and our pitchers gave out too many free passes. Also, we did not even need a hit with runners in scoring position. Many of those at-bats could have driven in the run by simply making contact. Our team did not deserve to win the game.

5. Which of the following best describes the main point of dispute between the reporter and baseball coach?
   a. Whether the loss was heartbreaking.
   b. Whether getting zero hits in twenty at-bats with runners in scoring position caused the loss.
   c. Numerous errors in the field and pitchers giving too many free passes caused the loss.
   d. Whether the team deserved to win the game.

Read the following exchange.

Conservative Politician: Social welfare programs are destroying our country. These programs are not only adding to the annual deficit, which increases the national debt, but they also discourage hard work. Our country must continue producing leaders who bootstrap their way to the top. None of our country's citizens truly *need* assistance from the government; rather, the assistance just makes things easier.

Liberal Politician: Our great country is founded on the principle of hope. The country is built on the backs of immigrants who came here with nothing, except for the hope of a better life. Our country is too wealthy not to provide basic necessities for the less fortunate. Recent immigrants, single mothers, historically disenfranchised, disabled persons, and the elderly all require an ample safety net.

6. What is the main point of dispute between the politicians?
   a. Spending on social welfare programs increases the national debt.
   b. Certain classes of people rely on social welfare programs to meet their basic needs.
   c. Certain classes of people would be irreparably harmed if the country failed to provide a social welfare program.
   d. All of the country's leaders have bootstrapped their way to the top.
   e. Immigrants founded the country.

Questions 7–13 are based on the following passage:

> In the quest to understand existence, modern philosophers must question if humans can fully comprehend the world. Classical western approaches to philosophy tend to hold that one can understand something, be it an event or object, by standing outside of the phenomena and observing it. It is then by unbiased observation that one can grasp the details of the world. This seems to hold true for many things. Scientists conduct experiments and record their findings, and thus many natural phenomena become comprehendible. However, several of these observations were possible because humans used tools in order to make these discoveries.
>
> This may seem like an extraneous matter. After all, people invented things like microscopes and telescopes in order to enhance their capacity to view cells or the movement of stars. While humans are still capable of seeing things, the question remains if human beings have the capacity to fully observe and see the world in order to understand it. It would not be an impossible stretch to argue that what humans see through a microscope is not the exact thing itself, but a human interpretation of it.
>
> This would seem to be the case in the "Business of the Holes" experiment conducted by Richard Feynman. To study the way electrons behave, Feynman set up a barrier with two holes and a plate. The plate was there to indicate how many times the electrons would pass through the hole(s). Rather than casually observe the electrons acting under normal circumstances, Feynman discovered that electrons behave in two totally different ways depending on whether or not they are observed. The electrons that were observed had passed through either one of the holes or were caught on the plate as particles. However, electrons that weren't observed acted as waves instead of particles and passed through both holes. This indicated that electrons have a dual nature. Electrons seen by the human eye act like particles, while unseen electrons act like waves of energy.

This dual nature of the electrons presents a conundrum. While humans now have a better understanding of electrons, the fact remains that people cannot entirely perceive how electrons behave without the use of instruments. We can only observe one of the mentioned behaviors, which only provides a partial understanding of the entire function of electrons. Therefore, we're forced to ask ourselves whether the world we observe is objective or if it is subjectively perceived by humans. Or, an alternative question: can man understand the world only through machines that will allow them to observe natural phenomena?

Both questions humble man's capacity to grasp the world. However, those ideas don't take into account that many phenomena have been proven by human beings without the use of machines, such as the discovery of gravity. Like all philosophical questions, whether man's reason and observation alone can understand the universe can be approached from many angles.

7. What is the author's motivation for writing the passage?
   a. Bring to light an alternative view on human perception by examining the role of technology in human understanding.
   b. Educate the reader on the latest astroparticle physics discovery and offer terms that may be unfamiliar to the reader.
   c. Argue that humans are totally blind to the realities of the world by presenting an experiment that proves that electrons are not what they seem on the surface.
   d. Reflect on opposing views of human understanding.

8. Which of the following most closely resembles the way in which paragraph four is structured?
   a. It offers one solution, questions the solution, and then ends with an alternative solution.
   b. It presents an inquiry, explains the detail of that inquiry, and then offers a solution.
   c. It presents a problem, explains the details of that problem, and then ends with more inquiry.
   d. It gives a definition, offers an explanation, and then ends with an inquiry.

9. For the classical approach to understanding to hold true, which of the following must be required?
   a. A telescope.
   b. The person observing must prove their theory beyond a doubt.
   c. Multiple witnesses present.
   d. The person observing must be unbiased.

10. Which best describes how the electrons in the experiment behaved like waves?
   a. The electrons moved up and down like actual waves.
   b. The electrons passed through both holes and then onto the plate.
   c. The electrons converted to photons upon touching the plate.
   d. Electrons were seen passing through one hole or the other.

11. The author mentions "gravity" in the last paragraph in order to do what?
   a. In order to show that different natural phenomena test man's ability to grasp the world.
   b. To prove that since man has not measured it with the use of tools or machines, humans cannot know the true nature of gravity.
   c. To demonstrate an example of natural phenomena humans discovered and understood without the use of tools or machines.
   d. To show an alternative solution to the nature of electrons that humans have not thought of yet.

12. Which situation best parallels the revelation of the dual nature of electrons discovered in Feynman's experiment?

   a. A man is born color-blind and grows up observing everything in lighter or darker shades. With the invention of special goggles he puts on, he discovers that there are other colors in addition to different shades.
   b. The coelacanth was thought to be extinct, but a live specimen was just recently discovered. There are now two living species of coelacanth known to man, and both are believed to be endangered.
   c. In the Middle Ages, blacksmiths added carbon to iron, thus inventing steel. The consequences of this important discovery would have its biggest effects during the industrial revolution.
   d. In order to better examine and treat broken bones, the x-ray machine was invented and put to use in hospitals and medical centers.

13. Which statement about technology would the author likely disagree with?

   a. Technology can help expand the field of human vision.
   b. Technology renders human observation irrelevant.
   c. Developing tools used in observation and research indicates growing understanding of our world in itself.
   d. Studying certain phenomena necessitates the use of tools and machines.

Question 14 is based on the following passage.

> In 2015, 28 countries, including Estonia, Portugal, Slovenia, and Latvia, scored significantly higher than the United States on standardized high school math tests. In the 1960s, the United States consistently ranked first in the world. Today, the United States spends more than $800 billion dollars on education, which exceeds the next highest country by more than $600 billion dollars. The United States also leads the world in spending per school-aged child by an enormous margin.

14. If these statements above are factual, which of the following statements must be correct?

   a. Outspending other countries on education has benefits beyond standardized math tests.
   b. The United States' education system is corrupt and broken.
   c. The standardized math tests are not representative of American academic prowess.
   d. Spending more money does not guarantee success on standardized math tests.

15. In 1889, Jerome K. Jerome wrote a humorous account of a boating holiday. Originally intended as a chapter in a serious travel guide, the work became a prime example of a comic novel. Read the passage below, noting the word/words in italics. Answer the question that follows.

> I felt rather hurt about this at first; it seemed somehow to be a sort of slight. Why hadn't I got housemaid's knee? Why this invidious reservation? After a while, however, less grasping feelings prevailed. I reflected that I had every other known malady in the pharmacology, and I grew less selfish, and determined to do without housemaid's knee. Gout, in its most malignant stage, it would appear, had seized me without my being aware of it; and *zymosis* I had evidently been suffering with from boyhood. There were no more diseases after *zymosis*, so I concluded there was nothing else the matter with me.

"Three Men in a Boat" by Jerome K. Jerome

Which definition best fits the word *zymosis*?

a. Discontent
b. An infectious disease
c. Poverty
d. Bad luck

Questions 16–25 are based on the following passage:

We made it. We created it. We brought it forth from the night of the ages. We alone. Our hands. Our mind. Ours alone and only.

We know not what we are saying. Our head is reeling. We look upon the light which we have made. We shall be forgiven for anything we say tonight...

Tonight, after more days and trials than we can count, we finished building a strange thing, from the remains of the Unmentionable Times, a box of glass, devised to give forth the power of the sky of greater strength than we had ever achieved before. And when we put our wires to this box, when we closed the current—the wire glowed! It came to life, it turned red, and a circle of light lay on the stone before us.

We stood, and we held our head in our hands. We could not conceive of that which we had created. We had touched no flint, made no fire. Yet here was light, light that came from nowhere, light from the heart of metal.

We blew out the candle. Darkness swallowed us. There was nothing left around us, nothing save night and a thin thread of flame in it, as a crack in the wall of a prison. We stretched our hands to the wire, and we saw our fingers in the red glow. We could not see our body nor feel it, and in that moment nothing existed save our two hands over a wire glowing in a black abyss.

Then we thought of the meaning of that which lay before us. We can light our tunnel, and the City, and all the Cities of the world with nothing save metal and wires. We can give our brothers a new light, cleaner and brighter than any they have ever known. The power of the sky can be made to do men's bidding. There are no limits to its secrets and its might, and it can be made to grant us anything if we but choose to ask.

Then we knew what we must do. Our discovery is too great for us to waste our time in sweeping the streets. We must not keep our secret to ourselves, nor buried under the ground. We must bring it into the sight of all men. We need all our time, we need the work rooms of the Home of the Scholars, we want the help of our brother Scholars and their wisdom joined to ours. There is so much work ahead for all of us, for all the Scholars of the world.

In a month, the World Council of Scholars is to meet in our City. It is a great Council, to which the wisest of all lands are elected, and it meets once a year in the different Cities of the earth. We shall go to this Council and we shall lay before them, as our gift, this glass box with the power of the sky. We shall confess everything to them. They will see, understand and forgive. For our gift is greater than our transgression. They will explain it to the Council of Vocations, and we shall be assigned to the Home of the Scholars. This has never been done before, but neither has a gift such as ours ever been offered to men.

We must wait. We must guard our tunnel as we had never guarded it before. For should any men save the Scholars learn of our secret, they would not understand it, nor would they believe us. They would see nothing, save our crime of working alone, and they would destroy us and our light. We care not about our body, but our light is...

Yes, we do care. For the first time do we care about our body. For this wire is as a part of our body, as a vein torn from us, glowing with our blood. Are we proud of this thread of metal, or of our hands which made it, or is there a line to divide these two?

Excerpt from *Anthem* by Ayn Rand

16. What is the overall tone of this passage?
    a. Dreary
    b. Unnerving
    c. Excited
    d. Humorous

17. Why must the invention be kept a secret?
    a. It is illegal to work alone.
    b. The Home of the Scholars will try to take credit.
    c. They were supposed to be sweeping streets.
    d. Remains from the Unmentionable Times are off limits.

18. Which literary device is used in the following sentence from paragraph five?
    Darkness swallowed us.

    a. Metaphor
    b. Synecdoche
    c. Flashback
    d. Personification

19. What does the narrator compare their discovery to?
    a. The sun
    b. A candle
    c. Prison
    d. Blood

20. Why does the narrator expect to be forgiven?
    a. Their invention will save the City money.
    b. The possibilities of the invention outweigh their crime.
    c. They will apologize to the World Council of Scholars.
    d. Their invention is part of their body.

21. What is the meaning of the word *transgression* mean in paragraph eight?
    a. Obedience
    b. Disruption
    c. Confession
    d. Offense

22. Which quote is an example of personification?
    a. "Our head is reeling."
    b. "Darkness swallowed us."
    c. "We stood, and we held our head in our hands."
    d. "We care not about our body, but our light is..."

23. What will NOT help advance the narrator's discovery?
    a. Using the work rooms of the Home of the Scholars
    b. Gaining wisdom from the brother Scholars
    c. Keeping the discovery a secret from the World Council of Scholars
    d. Stopping the sweeping of the streets

24. How does the narrator feel their status will change as a result of their invention?
    a. They will advance from street sweeper to the Home of the Scholars.
    b. Their status will remain the same after their confession.
    c. They will rise in status from tunnel worker to the Council of Vocations.
    d. They are not sure how their status will change due to the crime they committed.

25. Which transformation has happened by the end of the passage?
    a. The narrator has been forgiven for their transgression.
    b. The gift of electricity has been shared with all the cities of the world.
    c. The discovery has made it easier to sweep streets and light tunnels.
    d. The narrator recognizes the significance of their body.

26. When selecting a career path, it's important to explore the various options available. Many students entering college may shy away from a major because they don't know much about it. For example, many students won't opt for a career as an actuary, because they aren't exactly sure what it entails. But in doing so, they are missing out on a career that is very lucrative and in high demand. Actuaries work in the insurance field and assess risks and premiums. The average salary of an actuary is $100,000 per year. Another career option students may avoid, due to lack of knowledge of the field, is a hospitalist. This is a physician that specializes in the care of patients in a hospital, as opposed to those seen in private practices. The average salary of a hospitalist is upwards of $200,000. It pays to do some digging and find out more about these lesser-known career fields.
An actuary is:
    a. A doctor who works in a hospital
    b. The same as a hospitalist
    c. An insurance agent who works in a hospital
    d. A person who assesses insurance risks and premiums

Questions 27–36 are based on the following passage:

> In the quest to understand existence, modern philosophers must question if humans can fully comprehend the world. Classical western approaches to philosophy tend to hold that one can understand something, be it an event or object, by standing outside of the phenomena and observing it. It is then by unbiased observation that one can grasp the details of the world. This seems to hold true for many things. Scientists conduct experiments and record their findings, and thus many natural phenomena become comprehendible. However, several of these observations were possible because humans used tools in order to make these discoveries.

This may seem like an extraneous matter. After all, people invented things like microscopes and telescopes in order to enhance their capacity to view cells or the movement of stars. While humans are still capable of seeing things, the question remains if human beings have the capacity to fully observe and see the world in order to understand it. It would not be an impossible stretch to argue that what humans see through a microscope is not the exact thing itself, but a human interpretation of it.

This would seem to be the case in the "Business of the Holes" experiment conducted by Richard Feynman. To study the way electrons behave, Feynman set up a barrier with two holes and a plate. The plate was there to indicate how many times the electrons would pass through the hole(s). Rather than casually observe the electrons acting under normal circumstances, Feynman discovered that electrons behave in two totally different ways depending on whether or not they are observed. The electrons that were observed had passed through either one of the holes or were caught on the plate as particles. However, electrons that weren't observed acted as waves instead of particles and passed through both holes. This indicated that electrons have a dual nature. Electrons seen by the human eye act like particles, while unseen electrons act like waves of energy.

This dual nature of the electrons presents a conundrum. While humans now have a better understanding of electrons, the fact remains that people cannot entirely perceive how electrons behave without the use of instruments. We can only observe one of the mentioned behaviors, which only provides a partial understanding of the entire function of electrons. Therefore, we're forced to ask ourselves whether the world we observe is objective or if it is subjectively perceived by humans. Or, an alternative question: can man understand the world only through machines that will allow them to observe natural phenomena?

Both questions humble man's capacity to grasp the world. However, those ideas don't take into account that many phenomena have been proven by human beings without the use of machines, such as the discovery of gravity. Like all philosophical questions, whether man's reason and observation alone can understand the universe can be approached from many angles.

27. The word *extraneous* in paragraph two can be best interpreted as referring to which one of the following?
   a. Indispensable
   b. Bewildering
   c. Superfluous
   d. Exuberant

28. What is the author's motivation for writing the passage?
   a. Bring to light an alternative view on human perception by examining the role of technology in human understanding.
   b. Educate the reader on the latest astroparticle physics discovery and offer terms that may be unfamiliar to the reader.
   c. Argue that humans are totally blind to the realities of the world by presenting an experiment that proves that electrons are not what they seem on the surface.
   d. Reflect on opposing views of human understanding.

29. Which of the following most closely resembles the way in which paragraph four is structured?
    a. It offers one solution, questions the solution, and then ends with an alternative solution.
    b. It presents an inquiry, explains the detail of that inquiry, and then offers a solution.
    c. It presents a problem, explains the details of that problem, and then ends with more inquiry.
    d. It gives a definition, offers an explanation, and then ends with an inquiry.

30. For the classical approach to understanding to hold true, which of the following must be required?
    a. A telescope.
    b. The person observing must prove their theory beyond a doubt.
    c. Multiple witnesses present.
    d. The person observing must be unbiased.

31. Which best describes how the electrons in the experiment behaved like waves?
    a. The electrons moved up and down like actual waves.
    b. The electrons passed through both holes and then onto the plate.
    c. The electrons converted to photons upon touching the plate.
    d. Electrons were seen passing through one hole or the other.

32. The author mentions "gravity" in the last paragraph in order to do what?
    a. To show that different natural phenomena test man's ability to grasp the world.
    b. To prove that since man has not measured it with the use of tools or machines, humans cannot know the true nature of gravity.
    c. To demonstrate an example of natural phenomena humans discovered and understood without the use of tools or machines.
    d. To show an alternative solution to the nature of electrons that humans have not thought of yet.

33. Which situation best parallels the revelation of the dual nature of electrons discovered in Feynman's experiment?
    a. A man is born color-blind and grows up observing everything in lighter or darker shades. With the invention of special goggles he puts on, he discovers that there are other colors in addition to different shades.
    b. The coelacanth was thought to be extinct, but a live specimen was just recently discovered. There are now two living species of coelacanth known to man, and both are believed to be endangered.
    c. In the Middle Ages, blacksmiths added carbon to iron, thus inventing steel. The consequences of this important discovery would have its biggest effects during the industrial revolution.
    d. In order to better examine and treat broken bones, the x-ray machine was invented and put to use in hospitals and medical centers.

34. Which statement about technology would the author likely disagree with?
    a. Technology can help expand the field of human vision.
    b. Technology renders human observation irrelevant.
    c. Developing tools used in observation and research indicates growing understanding of our world itself.
    d. Studying certain phenomena necessitates the use of tools and machines.

35. As it is used in paragraph 4, the word *conundrum* most nearly means:
   a. platitude
   b. enigma
   c. solution
   d. hypothesis

36. What is the author's purpose in paragraph 3?
   a. To prove to the audience the thesis of the passage by providing evidence suggesting that electrons behave differently when observed by the human eye.
   b. To propose that the experiment conducted was not ethically done and to provide evidence that a new experiment should be conducted in order to reach the truth.
   c. To introduce the topic to the audience in a manner that puts it into a practical as well as historical understanding.
   d. To pose a question relating to the topic about whether humans fully observe phenomena in an objective or subjective sense.

Answer Explanations #3

Algebra and Functions

1. A: Parallel lines have the same slope. The slope of the given equation is 3. The slope of Choice *C* can be seen to be $\frac{1}{3}$ by dividing both sides by 3. The other choice are in standard form $Ax + By = C$, for which the slope is given by $\frac{-A}{B}$. For Choice *A*, the equation can be written as $6x - 2y = -2$. Therefore, the slope is:

$$\frac{-A}{B} = \frac{-6}{-2} = 3$$

This is the same as the given equation. The slope of Choice *B* is:

$$\frac{-A}{B} = \frac{-4}{-1} = 4$$

The slope of Choice *B* is 4. The slope of Choice *D* is:

$$\frac{-A}{B} = \frac{-2}{-2} = 1$$

2. D: For manufacturing costs, there is a linear relationship between the cost to the company and the number produced, with a *y*-intercept given by the base cost of acquiring the means of production and a slope given by the cost to produce one unit. In this case, that base cost is $50,000, while the cost per unit is $40. So:

$$y = 40x + 50{,}000$$

3. A: First solve for x, *y*, and *z*:

$$3x = 24$$

$$x = 8$$

$$6y = 24$$

$$y = 4$$

$$-2z = 24$$

$$z = -12$$

This means the equation would be $4(8)(4) + (-12)$, which equals 116.

4. A: The solid dot is located between -2 and -3, and the open dot is located between 1 and 2. Therefore, x is between -2.5 and 1.5, which can be converted to $-\frac{5}{2}$ and $\frac{3}{2}$. The solid dot indicates greater than or equal to, and the open dot indicates less than so the inequality is:

$$-\frac{5}{2} \leq x < \frac{3}{2}$$

5. C: Nothing is added to *x* and *y* since the center is 0 and 5^2 is 25. Choice *A* is not the correct answer because you do not subtract the radius from *x* and *y*. Choice *B* is not the correct answer because you must square the radius on the right side of the equation. Choice *D* is not the correct answer because you do not add the radius to x and y in the equation.

6. B: For an ordered pair to be a solution to a system of inequalities, it must make a true statement for BOTH inequalities when substituting its values for x and y. Substituting $(-3, -2)$ into the inequalities produces $(-2) > 2(-3) - 3$, which is $-2 > -9$, and $(-2) < -4(-3) + 8$, or $-2 < 20$. Both are true statements.

7. D: The shape of the scatterplot is a parabola (U-shaped). This eliminates Choices *A* (a linear equation that produces a straight line) and *C* (an exponential equation that produces a smooth curve upward or downward). The value of a for a quadratic function in standard form ($y = ax^2 + bx + c$) indicates whether the parabola opens up (U-shaped) or opens down (upside-down U). A negative value for a produces a parabola that opens down; therefore, Choice *B* can also be eliminated.

8. D: If $n = 2^2, n = 4$, and $m = 4^2 = 16$. This means that $m^n = 16^4$. This is the same as 2^{16}.

9. D: Each of the choices given is a linear function in the form of $y = mx + b$, where m is the slope, and b is the y-intercept. For the first function $g(x) = x - 4$, the slope is 1, and the y-intercept is -4. Placing this line on the graph would show that it does not intersect the absolute value function above. It crosses the y-axis at -4 with a slope equal to the right side of the absolute value graph, so the functions run parallel to one another.

The second function will intersect the graph at 1 point because the y-intercept is 0. The line will run parallel to the left side of the absolute value function, with a slope of -1. For the third function, the slope is 1, and the y-intercept is 2. It will cross the absolute value graph at 1 point because it runs parallel to the right side of the graph and runs through the y-axis at 2. The fourth function has a slope of ½ and a y-intercept of 0. This line will intersect the absolute value graph at exactly 2 points. One point is at $(2, 1)$, and the other point will be between x-values of -4 and -5.

This line is shown on the graph below:

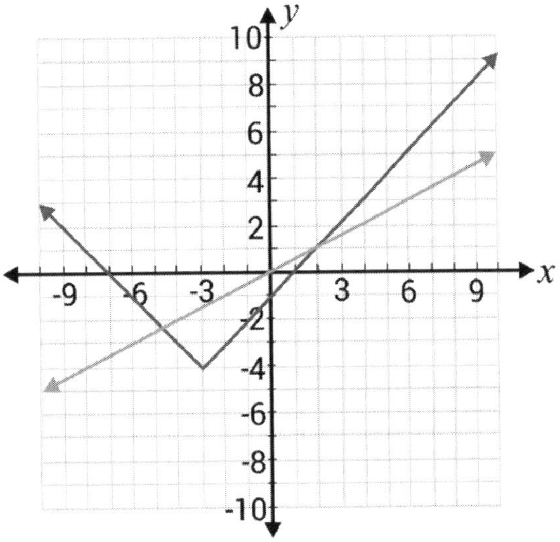

10. C: The value of $5h - 3$ cannot be a multiple of 5 because of the minus 3 at the end of the expression. Multiplying h by 5 yields a multiple of 5, but subtracting 3 means the final answer will no longer be a multiple of 5. For $10h + 20$, both the number multiplied by h and the number added to h are divisible by 5. The result will always be divisible by 5. For the final expression $h^3 + 6$, the value of h cubed yields an answer divisible by 5, but the addition of 6 means the answer is no longer divisible by 5.

11. D: The first step is to find the equation of the line that is perpendicular to $y = 2x - 3$ and passes through the point $(0, 5)$. The slope of a perpendicular line is found by the negative reciprocal of 2, which is $-\frac{1}{2}$. The y-intercept is the value of y when $x = 0$, so the y-intercept is 5.

The new equation is $y = -\frac{1}{2}x + 5$.

In order to find which points lie on the new line, the values of x and y can be substituted into the equation to determine if they form a true statement.

For the point in *A*, the equation $10 = -\frac{1}{2}(-6) + 5$ makes the statement $10 = 8$.

This is not a true statement, so the point $(-6, 10)$ does not lie on the line.

For *B*, the equation $7 = -\frac{1}{2}(-2) + 5$ makes the statement $7 = 6$, which is not a true statement.

Therefore, Choice *B* is not a point that lies on the line.

For Choice *C*, the equation $6 = -\frac{1}{2}(2) + 5$ is the same as $6 = 4$, so it is similarly false.

For *D*, the equation $3 = -\frac{1}{2}(4) + 5$ makes a true statement, so the point $(4, 3)$ lies on the line.

12. B: To simplify the given expression, the first step is to make all exponents positive by moving them to the opposite place in the fraction. This expression becomes:

$$\frac{4b^3b^2}{a^1a^4} \times \frac{3a}{b}$$

Then the rules for exponents can be used to simplify. Multiplying the same bases means the exponents can be added. Dividing the same bases means the exponents are subtracted. Thus, after multiplying the exponents in the first fraction, the equation becomes:

$$\frac{4b^5}{a^5} \times \frac{3a}{b}$$

Therefore, we can first multiply to get:

$$\frac{12ab^5}{a^5b}$$

Then, simplifying yields:

$$12\frac{b^4}{a^4}$$

13. D: The expression is three times the sum of twice a number and 1, which is $3(2x + 1)$. Then, 6 is subtracted from this expression.

14. A: Robert accomplished his task on Tuesday in $\frac{3}{4}$ the time compared to Monday. He must have worked $\frac{4}{3}$ as fast.

15. D: The slope from this equation is 50, and it is interpreted as the cost per gigabyte used. Since the g-value represents number of gigabytes and the equation is set equal to the cost in dollars, the slope relates these two values. For every gigabyte used on the phone, the bill goes up 50 dollars.

16. C: Because the triangles are similar, the lengths of the corresponding sides are proportional. Therefore:

$$\frac{30 + x}{30} = \frac{22}{14} = \frac{y + 15}{y}$$

This results in the equation:

$$14(30 + x) = 22 \times 30$$

When solved, this gives:

$$x = 17.1$$

The proportion also results in the equation:

$$14(y + 15) = 22y$$

When solved, this gives:

$$y = 26.3$$

17. C: The quadratic formula can be used to solve this problem. Given the equation, use the values $a = 1$, $b = -2$, and $c = 8$.

$$x = \frac{-b \pm \sqrt{b^2 - 4ac}}{2a} = \frac{-(-2) \pm \sqrt{(-2)^2 - 4(1)(-8)}}{2(1)}$$

From here, simplify to solve for x.

$$x = \frac{2 \pm \sqrt{4 + 32}}{2} = \frac{2 \pm \sqrt{36}}{2} = \frac{2 \pm 6}{2} = 1 \pm 3$$

18. B: To factor $x^2 + 4x + 4$, the numbers needed are those that add to 4 and multiply to 4. Therefore, both numbers must be 2, and the expression factors to:

$$x^2 + 4x + 4 = (x + 2)^2$$

Similarly, in order for both to have $x + 2$ in common, the second expression factors to:

$$x^2 - x - 6 = (x - 3)(x + 2)$$

19. D: This system of equations involves one quadratic function and one linear function, as seen from the degree of each equation. One way to solve this is through substitution.

Solving for y in the second equation yields:

$$y = x + 2$$

Plugging this equation in for the y of the quadratic equation yields:

$$x^2 - 2x + x + 2 = 8$$

Simplifying the equation, it becomes:

$$x^2 - x + 2 = 8$$

Setting this equal to zero and factoring, it becomes:

$$x^2 - x - 6 = 0 = (x - 3)(x + 2)$$

Solving these two factors for x gives the zeros:

$$x = 3, -2$$

To find the y-value for the point, each number can be plugged in to either original equation. Solving each one for y yields the points $(3, 5)$ and $(-2, 0)$.

20. D: The midpoint formula should be used to get the average of both points.

$$M = \left(\frac{x_1 + x_2}{2}, \frac{y_1 + y_2}{2}\right) = \left(\frac{-1+3}{2}, \frac{2+(-6)}{2}\right) = (1, -2)$$

21. A: First, the sample mean must be calculated.

$$\bar{x} = \frac{1}{4}(1+3+5+7) = 4$$

The sample standard deviation of the data set is:

$$s = \sqrt{\frac{\sum(x-\bar{x})^2}{n-1}}$$

$n = 4$ represents the number of data points.

Therefore, the sample standard deviation is:

$$s = \sqrt{\frac{1}{3}[(1-4)^2 + (3-4)^2 + (5-4)^2 + (7-4)^2]}$$

$$s = \sqrt{\frac{1}{3}(9+1+1+9)} = 2.58$$

22. D: The slope is given by the change in y divided by the change in x. The change in y is $2 - 0 = 2$, and the change in x is:

$$0 - (-4) = 4$$

The slope is $\frac{2}{4} = \frac{1}{2}$.

23. C: Janice will be choosing 4 employees out of a set of 6 applicants, so this will be given by the choice function. The following equation shows the choice function worked out:

$$\binom{6}{4} = \frac{6!}{4!\,(6-4)!} = \frac{6!}{4!\,(2)!}$$

$$\frac{6 \cdot 5 \cdot 4 \cdot 3 \cdot 2 \cdot 1}{4 \cdot 3 \cdot 2 \cdot 1 \cdot 2 \cdot 1} = \frac{6 \cdot 5}{2} = 15$$

24. C: The $(3x+1)$ can be factored to get $(2x-5)(3x+1)$.

25. D: Because the coefficient of x^2 is negative, this function has a graph that is a parabola that opens downward. Therefore, it will be greater than 0 between its real roots, if it has any. Checking the discriminant, the result is:

$$1^2 - 4(-3)(-8) = 1 - 96 = -95$$

Since the discriminant is negative, this equation has no real solutions. Since this has no real roots, it must be always positive or always negative. Its graph opens downward, so it has at least some negative values. That means it is always negative. Thus, it is greater than zero for no real numbers.

26. A: Check each value, but it is easiest to use the quadratic formula, which gives

$$x = \frac{2 \pm \sqrt{(-2)^2 - 4(1)(-2)}}{2} = 1 \pm \frac{\sqrt{12}}{2}$$

$$1 \pm \frac{2\sqrt{3}}{2} = 1 \pm \sqrt{3}$$

The only one of these which appears as an answer choice is $1 + \sqrt{3}$.

27. B: The graph of $y = x^2 + 2$ has a vertex at (0, 2) on the *y*-axis. The circle with a center at (0, 1) also lies on the *y*-axis. With a radius of 1, the circle touches the parabola at one point: the vertex of the parabola (0, 2).

28. A: Finding the roots means finding the values of *x* when *y* is zero. The quadratic formula could be used, but in this case, it is possible to factor by hand, since the numbers -1 and 2 add to 1 and multiply to -2. So, factor $x^2 + x - 2 = (x - 1)(x + 2) = 0$, then set each factor equal to zero. Solving for each value gives the values *x* = 1 and *x* = -2.

29. D: The first field has an area of 1,000 feet, so the length of one side is $\sqrt{1{,}000} = 10\sqrt{10}$. Since there are four sides to a square, the total perimeter is $40\sqrt{10}$. The second square has an area of 10 square feet, so the length of one side is $\sqrt{10}$, and the total perimeter is $4\sqrt{10}$. Adding these together gives $40\sqrt{10} + 4\sqrt{10} = (40 + 4)\sqrt{10} = 44\sqrt{10}$.

30. B: The number of ways to order *n* objects is given by the product $\binom{n}{1}\binom{n-1}{1}\dots\binom{1}{1}$. This is $\binom{3}{1}\binom{2}{1}\binom{1}{1} = \frac{3!}{1!2!} \times \frac{2!}{1!1!} \times \frac{1!}{1!1!}$. $1!$ is just 1, and the $2!$ in the numerator and denominator will cancel one another, with a result of $3! = 3 \times 2 \times 1 = 6$.

31. C: Find $a_2 = 3a_1 - 1 = 3 \times 1 - 1 = 2$. Next, find $a_3 = 3a_2 - 1 = 3 \times 2 - 1 = 5$.

32. C: Each number in the sequence is adding one more than the difference between the previous two.

For example, $10 - 6 = 4, 4 + 1 = 5$.

Therefore, the next number after 10 is $10 + 5 = 15$.

Going forward, $21 - 15 = 6, 6 + 1 = 7$. The next number is $21 + 7 = 28$.

Therefore, the difference between numbers is the set of whole numbers starting at 2: 2, 3, 4, 5, 6, 7....

33. B: This is a division problem because the original amount needs to be split up into equal amounts. The mixed number $11\frac{1}{2}$ should be converted to an improper fraction first:

$$11\frac{1}{2} = \frac{(11 \times 2) + 1}{2} = \frac{23}{2}$$

Carey needs to determine how many times $\frac{23}{2}$ goes into 184. This is a division problem:

$$184 \div \frac{23}{2} = ?$$

The fraction can be flipped, and the problem turns into the multiplication:

$$184 \times \frac{2}{23} = \frac{368}{23}$$

This improper fraction can be simplified into 16 because $368 \div 23 = 16$. The answer is 16 lawn segments.

Reading Comprehension

1. B: The passage indicates that Annabelle has a fear of going outside into the daylight. Thus *heliophobia* must refer to a fear of bright lights or sunlight. Choice *B* is the only answer that describes this.

2. D: Although Washington was from a wealthy background, the passage does not say that his wealth led to his republican ideals, so Choice *A* is not supported. Choice *B* also does not follow from the passage. Washington's warning against meddling in foreign affairs does not mean that he would oppose wars of every kind, so Choice *B* is wrong. Choice *C* is also unjustified since the author does not indicate that Alexander Hamilton's assistance was absolutely necessary. Choice *D* is correct because the farewell address clearly opposes political parties and partisanship. The author then notes that presidential elections often hit a fever pitch of partisanship. Thus, it follows that George Washington would not approve of modern political parties and their involvement in presidential elections.

3. A: The author finishes the passage by applying Washington's farewell address to modern politics, so the purpose probably includes this application. Choice *B* is wrong because George Washington is already a well-established historical figure; furthermore, the passage does not seek to introduce him. Choice *C* is wrong because the author is not fighting a common perception that Washington was merely a military hero. Choice *D* is wrong because the author is not convincing readers. Persuasion does not correspond to the passage. Choice *A* states the primary purpose.

4. D: Choice *A* is wrong because the last paragraph is not appropriate for a history textbook. Choice *B* is false because the piece is not a notice or announcement of Washington's death. Choice *C* is clearly false because it is not fiction, but a historical writing. Choice *D* is correct. The passage is most likely to appear in a newspaper editorial because it cites information relevant and applicable to the present day, a popular format in editorials.

5. B: Choice *A* uses similar language, but it is not the main point of disagreement. The reporter calls the loss devastating, and there's no reason to believe that the coach would disagree with this assessment. Eliminate this choice. Choice *B* is strong since both passages mention the at-bats with runners in scoring position. The reporter asserts that the team lost due to the team failing to get such a hit. In contrast, the coach identifies several other reasons for the loss, including fielding and pitching errors. Additionally, the coach disagrees that the team even needed a hit in those situations. Choice *C* is mentioned by the coach, but not by the reporter. It is unclear whether the reporter would agree with this assessment. Eliminate this choice. Choice *D* is mentioned by the coach but not by the reporter. It is not stated whether the reporter believes that the team deserved to win. Eliminate this choice. Therefore, Choice *B* is the correct answer.

6. C: Choice *A* is incorrect. The Conservative Politician definitely believes that spending on social welfare programs increases the national debt. However, the Liberal Politician does not address the cost of those programs. Choice *B* is a strong answer choice. The Liberal Politician explicitly agrees that certain classes of people rely on social welfare programs. The Conservative Politician actually agrees that people rely on the programs, but thinks this reliance is detrimental. This answer choice is slightly off base. Eliminate this choice. Choice *C* improves on Choice *B*. The Liberal Politician definitely believes that certain classes of people would be irreparably harmed. In contrast, the Conservative Politician asserts that the programs are actually harmful since people become dependent on the programs. The Conservative Politician concludes that people don't need the assistance and would be better off if left to fend for themselves. This is definitely the main point of disagreement. Choice *D* is not the main point of dispute.

Neither of the politicians discusses whether *all* of the nation's leaders have bootstrapped their way to the top. Eliminate this choice.

7. A: Bring to light an alternative view on human perception by examining the role of technology in human understanding. This is a challenging question because the author's purpose is somewhat open-ended. The author concludes by stating that the questions regarding human perception and observation can be approached from many angles. Thus they do not seem to be attempting to prove one thing or another. Choice *B* is incorrect because we cannot know for certain whether the electron experiment is the latest discovery in astroparticle physics because no date is given. Choice *C* is a broad generalization that does not reflect accurately on the writer's views. While the author does appear to reflect on opposing views of human understanding (Choice *D*), the best answer is Choice *A*.

8. C: It presents a problem, explains the details of that problem, and then ends with more inquiry. The beginning of this paragraph literally "presents a conundrum," explains the problem of partial understanding, and then ends with more questions, or inquiry. There is no solution offered in this paragraph, making Choices *A* and *B* incorrect. Choice *D* is incorrect because the paragraph does not begin with a definition.

9. D: Looking back in the text, the author describes that classical philosophy holds that understanding can be reached by careful observation. This will not work if they are overly invested or biased in their pursuit. Choices *A* and *C* are in no way related and are completely unnecessary. A specific theory is not necessary to understanding, according to classical philosophy mentioned by the author. Again, the key to understanding is observing the phenomena outside of it, without bias or predisposition. Thus, Choice *B* is wrong.

10. B: The electrons passed through both holes and then onto the plate. Choices *A* and *C* are incorrect because such movement is not mentioned at all in the text. In the passage, the author says that electrons that were physically observed appeared to pass through one hole or another. Remember, the electrons that were observed doing this were described as acting like particles. Therefore, Choice *D* is incorrect. Recall that the plate actually recorded electrons passing through both holes simultaneously and hitting the plate. This behavior, the electron activity that wasn't seen by humans, was characteristic of waves. Thus, Choice *B* is the correct answer.

11. C: To demonstrate an example of natural phenomena humans discovered and understood without the use of tools or machines. Choice *A* mirrors the language in the beginning of the paragraph but is incorrect in its intent. Choice *B* is incorrect; the paragraph mentions nothing of "not knowing the true nature of gravity." Choice *D* is incorrect as well. There is no mention of an "alternative solution" in this paragraph.

12. A: The important thing to keep in mind is that we must choose a scenario that best parallels, or is most similar to, the discovery of the experiment mentioned in the passage. The important aspects of the experiment can be summed up like so: humans directly observed one behavior of electrons and then through analyzing a tool (the plate that recorded electron hits), discovered that there was another electron behavior that could not be physically seen by human eyes. This best parallels the scenario in Choice *A*. Like Feynman, the colorblind person is able to observe one aspect of the world but through the special goggles (a tool) he is able to see a natural phenomenon that he could not physically see on his own. While Choice *D* is compelling, the x-ray helps humans see the broken bone, not necessarily revealing that the bone is broken in the first place. The other choices do not parallel the scenario in question. Therefore, Choice *A* is the best choice.

13. B: The author would not agree that technology renders human observation irrelevant. Choice *A* is incorrect because much of the passage discusses how technology helps humans observe what cannot be seen with the naked eye, therefore the author would agree with this statement. This line of reasoning is also why the author would agree with Choice *D*, making it incorrect as well. As indicated in the second paragraph, the author seems to think that humans create inventions and tools with the goal of studying phenomena more precisely. This indicates increased understanding as people recognize limitations and develop items to help bypass the limitations and learn. Therefore, Choice *C* is incorrect as well. Again, the author doesn't attempt to disprove or dismiss classical philosophy.

14. D: Outspending other countries on education could have other benefits, but there is no reference to this in the passage, so Choice *A* is incorrect. Choice *B* is incorrect because the author does not mention corruption. Choice *C* is incorrect because there is nothing in the passage stating that the tests are not genuinely representative. Choice *D* is accurate because spending more money has not brought success. The United States already spends the most money, and the country is not excelling on these tests. Choice *D* is the correct answer.

15. B: The correct answer is an infectious disease. By reading and understanding the context of the passage, all other options can be eliminated since the author restates zymosis as a disease.

16. C: There is a tone of excitement throughout the passage; this tone is conveyed through the narrator's account of the life-changing discovery of electricity. Mentions of tunnels and darkness could evoke a tone of dreariness, but that represents the past. This passage is looking forward to what the future will hold with this new form of light, making Choice *A* incorrect. Choice *B* is incorrect because the narrator does not feel unnerved when about the idea of confessing their crime to the Council. This passage does not use humor or lightheartedness, making Choice *D* incorrect.

17. A: Evidence for the correct answer can be found here: "They would see nothing, save our crime of working alone, and they would destroy us and our light." In this society, things must be done as a collective, not individually. The narrator hopes to join the Home of the Scholars, and wants their input and work space, which makes Choice *B* incorrect. Street sweeping is the narrator's role but it's not what makes their discovery a crime. That is why Choice *C* is incorrect. Besides the word *Unmentionable*, nothing indicates that remainders from former times are off-limits, making Choice *D* incorrect.

18. D: The sentence uses personification, whereby darkness is given a human quality—being able to swallow. There is no comparison being made, making metaphor, Choice *A*, incorrect. Synecdoche, which is a device that uses a part to represent a whole or vice versa is not present, making Choice *B* incorrect. The sentence has no interjected scenes from a previous point in the narrative, making flashback, Choice *C*, incorrect.

19. A: Multiple times the narrator calls their discovery "the power of the sky" which is an allusion to the sun. For example, in the third paragraph, the narrator reports, "we finished building a strange thing…a box of glass, devised to give forth the power of the sky of greater strength than we had ever achieved before." Candles were a source of light before this discovery, making Choice *B* incorrect. Prison represents the darkness, not the light, making Choice *C* incorrect. The narrator does feel that their invention is a part of their body, the way blood runs through their veins, but does not directly equate to their overall invention of electricity. This makes Choice *D* incorrect.

20. B: The narrator is confident their crime will be forgiven by the World Council of Scholars, because their "gift is greater than [their] transgression." The passage does not address the money their invention will save the City, making Choice *A* incorrect. It is not the apology alone that will grant the narrator forgiveness, making Choice *C* incorrect. By the end, the narrator does feel a strong connection to their invention, but the wires are only metaphorically part of their body, and the wires are not the reason the narrator believes they'll be forgiven. This makes Choice *D* incorrect.

21. D: *Transgression* most closely means *offense* in paragraph eight. Obedience, or following the rules, is the opposite of transgression, making Choice *A* incorrect. The word *transgression* has a moral or legal connotation that is lacking in the more abstract word *disruption*, making Choice *B* incorrect. Confession, or admitting to an offense, is what the narrator is going to do as a result of their transgression, making Choice *D* incorrect.

22. B: Personification is a literary device in which human characteristics are attributed to something nonhuman. So, when the narrator says "darkness swallowed us," they give a human characteristic (swallowing) to something nonhuman (darkness). Choice *A* is incorrect because it is just an expression used to indicate there are a lot of thoughts swirling around in the narrator's head. Choice *C* refers to the human narrator's head and hands; since the narrator is a person, they cannot be personified. Choice *D* is incorrect because it is a thought that trails off using ellipsis, not personification, to indicate that the narrator has changed their opinion on the value of their body.

23. C: The narrator wants to keep their invention a secret until they are able to confess everything to the World Council of Scholars. Paragraph seven lists the resources that are necessary to advance the discovery. Those include work rooms, which makes Choice *A* incorrect. The narrator also wants help and wisdom from the brother Scholars, making Choice *B* incorrect. The narrator feels that they will need to focus all their time on their discovery, which means they will need to stop sweeping the streets, leaving Choice *D* incorrect.

24. A: Moving from street sweeper to the Home of the Scholars will be an advancement in society. This is apparent because the narrator currently lives in a tunnel with no electricity, while the wisest in all the lands are elected to the World Council of Scholars. Choice *B* is incorrect because the text indicates that being a Scholar is more desirable than being a street sweeper, so their status will not remain the same. The Council of Vocations decides what jobs people will have, and would be the group to assign the narrator to the House of Scholars. This makes Choice *C* incorrect. The narrator is not concerned with the negative consequences of their confession and is confident they will be propelled to Scholar status. This is why Choice *D* is incorrect.

25. D: The last paragraph reveals the shift in how the narrator suddenly cares about their body for the first time after they discover electricity. The passage cuts off before the author shares whether the transgression is forgiven, making Choice *A* incorrect. The plan is to share the gift of electricity with all the Cities, but the reader does not know if that plan will come to fruition. This makes Choice *B* incorrect. It's likely that electricity will make all tasks, especially those that happen at night, easier. But Choice *C* is incorrect because those benefits are not discussed in this passage.

26. D: An actuary assesses risks and sets insurance premiums. While an actuary does work in insurance, the passage does not suggest that actuaries have any affiliation with hospitalists or working in a hospital, so all other choices are incorrect.

27. C: *Extraneous* most nearly means *superfluous*, or *trivial*. Choice *A, indispensable*, is incorrect because it means the opposite of *extraneous*. Choice *B, bewildering*, means *confusing* and is not relevant to the context of the sentence. Finally, Choice *D* is incorrect because although the prefix of the word is the same, ex-, the word exuberant means elated or enthusiastic, and is irrelevant to the context of the sentence.

28. A: Bring to light an alternative view on human perception by examining the role of technology in human understanding. This is a challenging question because the author's purpose is somewhat open-ended. The author concludes by stating that the questions regarding human perception and observation can be approached from many angles. Thus, they do not seem to be attempting to prove one thing or another. Choice *B* is incorrect because we cannot know for certain whether the electron experiment is the latest discovery in astroparticle physics because no date is given. Choice *C* is a broad generalization that does not reflect accurately on the writer's views. While the author does appear to reflect on opposing views of human understanding, Choice *D*, the best answer is Choice *A*.

29. C: It presents a problem, explains the details of that problem, and then ends with more inquiry. The beginning of this paragraph literally "presents a conundrum," explains the problem of partial understanding, and then ends with more questions, or inquiry. There is no solution offered in this paragraph, making Choices *A* and *B* incorrect. Choice *D* is incorrect because the paragraph does not begin with a definition.

30. D: Looking back in the text, the author describes that classical philosophy holds that understanding can be reached by careful observation. This will not work if they are overly invested or biased in their pursuit. Choices *A* and *C* are in no way related and are completely unnecessary. A specific theory is not necessary to understanding, according to classical philosophy mentioned by the author. Again, the key to understanding is observing the phenomena outside of it, without bias or predisposition. Thus, Choice *B* is wrong.

31. B: The electrons passed through both holes and then onto the plate. Choices *A* and *C* are incorrect because such movement is not mentioned at all in the text. In the passage, the author says that electrons that were physically observed appeared to pass through one hole or another. Remember, the electrons that were observed doing this were described as acting like particles. Therefore, Choice *D* is incorrect. Recall that the plate actually recorded electrons passing through both holes simultaneously and hitting the plate. This behavior, the electron activity that wasn't seen by humans, was characteristic of waves. Thus, Choice *B* is the correct answer.

32. C: The author mentions "gravity" to demonstrate an example of natural phenomena humans discovered and understood without the use of tools or machines. Choice *A* mirrors the language in the beginning of the paragraph but is incorrect in its intent. Choice *B* is incorrect; the paragraph mentions nothing of "not knowing the true nature of gravity." Choice *D* is incorrect as well. There is no mention of an "alternative solution" in this paragraph.

33. A: The important thing to keep in mind is that we must choose a scenario that best parallels, or is most similar to, the discovery of the experiment mentioned in the passage. The important aspects of the experiment can be summed up like so: humans directly observed one behavior of electrons and then through analyzing a tool (the plate that recorded electron hits), discovered that there was another electron behavior that could not be physically seen by human eyes. This summary best parallels the scenario in Choice *A*. Like Feynman, the colorblind person can observe one aspect of the world but through the special goggles (a tool), he is able to see a natural phenomenon that he could not physically see on his own. While Choice *D* is compelling, the x-ray helps humans see the broken bone, but it does not necessarily reveal that the bone is broken in the first place. The other choices do not parallel the scenario in question. Therefore, Choice *A* is the best choice.

34. B: The author would not agree that technology renders human observation irrelevant. Choice *A* is incorrect because much of the passage discusses how technology helps humans observe what cannot be seen with the naked eye; therefore, the author would agree with this statement. This line of reasoning is also why the author would agree with Choice *D,* making it incorrect as well. As indicated in the second paragraph, the author seems to think that humans create inventions and tools with the goal of studying phenomena more precisely. This indicates increased understanding as people recognize limitations and develop items to help bypass the limitations and learn. Therefore, Choice *C* is incorrect as well. Again, the author doesn't attempt to disprove or dismiss classical philosophy.

35. B: The word *conundrum* most nearly means *enigma,* which is a mystery or riddle. *Platitude* means a banal or overused saying. *Solution* is incorrect here; and *hypothesis* implies a theory or assumption, so this is also incorrect.

36. A: To prove to the audience the thesis of the passage by providing evidence suggesting that electrons behave differently when observed by the human eye. The thesis' best evidence is found in this paragraph because of the experiment depicting how electrons behave in a dual nature. Choice *B* is incorrect; the paragraph mentions nothing about the experiment being unethical. Choice *C* is incorrect; this is characteristic of the first paragraph. Choice *D* is incorrect; this is more characteristic of the second paragraph.

Dear IBEW Aptitude Test Taker,

Thank you again for purchasing this study guide for your ASWB Bachelors exam. We hope that we exceeded your expectations.

Our goal in creating this study guide was to cover all of the topics that you will see on the test. We also strove to make our practice questions as similar as possible to what you will encounter on test day. With that being said, if you found something that you feel was not up to your standards, please send us an email and let us know.

We would also like to let you know about other books in our catalog that may interest you.

ASWB Masters

This can be found on Amazon: amazon.com/dp/1637752849

ASWB Clinical

amazon.com/dp/1637756828

We have study guides in a wide variety of fields. If the one you are looking for isn't listed above, then try searching for it on Amazon or send us an email.

Thanks Again and Happy Testing!
Product Development Team
info@studyguideteam.com

FREE Test Taking Tips Video/DVD Offer

To better serve you, we created videos covering test taking tips that we want to give you for FREE. **These videos cover world-class tips that will help you succeed on your test.**

We just ask that you send us feedback about this product. Please let us know what you thought about it—whether good, bad, or indifferent.

To get your **FREE videos**, you can use the QR code below or email freevideos@studyguideteam.com with "Free Videos" in the subject line and the following information in the body of the email:

a. The title of your product

b. Your product rating on a scale of 1-5, with 5 being the highest

c. Your feedback about the product

If you have any questions or concerns, please don't hesitate to contact us at info@studyguideteam.com.

Thank you!

SCAN HERE

Made in the USA
Middletown, DE
04 November 2024

63858122R00099